Complexity and postmodernism

Complexity and Postmodernism explores the notion of complexity in the light of contemporary perspectives from philosophy and science. Paul Cilliers contributes to our general understanding of complex systems, and explores the implications of complexity theory for our understanding of biological and social systems. Postmodern theory is reinterpreted in order to argue that a postmodern perspective does not necessarily imply relativism, but that it could also be viewed as a manifestation of an inherent sensitivity to complexity.

As Cilliers explains, the characterisation of complexity revolves around analyses of the process of self-organisation and a rejection of traditional notions of representation. The model of language developed by Saussure – and expanded by Derrida – is used to develop the notion of distributed representation, which in turn is linked with distributed modelling techniques. Connectionism (implemented in neural networks) serves as an example of these techniques. Cilliers points out that this approach to complexity leads to models of complex systems that avoid the oversimplification that results from rule-based models.

Complexity and Postmodernism integrates insights from complexity and computational theory with the philosophical position of thinkers like Derrida and Lyotard. Cilliers takes a critical stance towards the use of the analytical method as a tool to cope with complexity, and he rejects Searle's superficial contribution to the debate.

Complexity and Postmodernism is an exciting and an original book that should be read by anyone interested in gaining a fresh understanding of complexity, postmodernism and connectionism.

Paul Cilliers lectures in philosophy at the University of Stellenbosch, South Africa. He worked as a research engineer for over a decade, specialising in computer modelling.

Complexity and postmodernism
Understanding complex systems

Paul Cilliers

London and New York

First published 1998
by Routledge
2 Park Square, Milton Park, Abingdon, Oxon, OX14 4RN

Simultaneously published in the USA and Canada
by Routledge
270 Madison Ave, New York NY 10016

Reprinted 1999, 2000

Transferred to Digital Printing 2005

Routledge is an imprint of the Taylor & Francis Group

© 1998 Paul Cilliers

Typeset in Times by Routledge

British Library Cataloguing in Publication Data
A catalogue record for this book is available from the British Library

Library of Congress Cataloguing in Publication Data
A catalogue record for this book has been requested

ISBN 0–415–15286–0 (hbk)
ISBN 0–415–15287–9 (pbk)

For Ilana and Cornel

Contents

Preface

'Complexity' and 'postmodernism' are both controversial notions. Contemporary society is readily described as being postmodern, but reactions to this description diverge sharply. For some (like Zygmunt Bauman) postmodernism creates the possibility to escape from the strictures of modernism and to re-enchant the world. For others (like Ernest Gellner) it exemplifies relativism – a theoretical framework in which anything goes – and leaves them with a feeling of vertigo. Postmodernism can also be seen as being parasitic on modernism, or as modernism's underbelly. In such a case it could be argued that we should drop the concept altogether if we want to move beyond the oversimplified ideals of the Enlightenment.

The different responses to postmodernism are based on different understandings of the word's meaning. Even if it were possible to clarify this debate, it is not my intention to do so in this book; nor shall I attempt to provide an apology for postmodernism. My main concern is with the notions of complexity and complex systems. As far as postmodernism is concerned, the argument is simply that a number of theoretical approaches, loosely (or even incorrectly) bundled together under the term 'postmodern' (e.g. those of Derrida and Lyotard), have an implicit sensitivity for the complexity of the phenomena they deal with. Instead of trying to analyse complex phenomena in terms of single or essential principles, these approaches acknowledge that it is not possible to tell a single and exclusive story about something that is really complex. The acknowledgement of complexity, however, certainly does *not* lead to the conclusion that anything goes.

The concept 'complexity' is not univocal either. Firstly, it is useful to distinguish between the notions 'complex' and 'complicated'. If a system – despite the fact that it may consist of a huge number of components – can be given a complete description in terms of its individual constituents, such a system is merely *complicated*. Things like jumbo jets or computers are complicated. In a *complex* system, on the other hand, the interaction among constituents of the system, and the interaction between the system and its environment, are of such a nature that the system as a whole cannot be fully understood simply by analysing its components. Moreover, these relationships are not fixed, but shift and change, often as a result of self-organisation. This can result in novel features, usually referred to in terms of *emergent properties*. The brain, natural language and social systems are complex. The problem of understanding this kind of complexity is a central issue throughout the book.

Secondly, it is necessary to say something about the relationship between complexity and chaos theory. The hype created by chaos theory has abated somewhat, but the perception that it has an important role to play in the study of complex systems is still widespread. Although I would not deny that chaos theory could contribute to the study of complexity, I do feel that its contribution would be extremely limited. When analysing complex systems, a sensitivity to initial conditions, for example, is not such an important issue. As a matter of fact, it is exactly the *robust* nature of complex systems, i.e. their capability to perform in the same way under different conditions, that ensures their survival. Although the metaphor of the butterfly's flapping wings causing a tornado on the other side of the globe is a good one for describing a sensitivity to initial conditions, it has caused so much confusion that I feel it should not be used at all. Chaotic behaviour – in the technical sense of 'deterministic chaos' – results from the non-linear interaction of a relatively small number of equations. In complex systems, however, there are always a huge number of interacting components. Despite the claims made about aspects of the functioning of the olfactory system, or of the heart in fibrillation, I am unsure whether any behaviour found in nature could be described as truly chaotic in the technical sense. Where sharp transitions between different states of a system are required, I find the notion of self-organised criticality (see Chapter 6) more appropriate than metaphors drawn from chaos. This might sound too dismissive, and I certainly do not want to claim that aspects of chaos theory (or fractal mathematics) cannot be used effectively in the process of modelling nature. My claim is rather that chaos theory, and especially the notions of deterministic chaos and universality, does not really help us to understand the dynamics of complex systems. That showpiece of fractal mathematics, the Mandelbrot set – sometimes referred to as the most complex mathematical object we know – is in the final analysis complicated, not complex. Within the framework of the present study, chaos theory is still part of the modern paradigm, and will not receive detailed attention.

The objective of the book is to illuminate the notion of complexity from a postmodern, or perhaps more accurately, *post-structural* perspective. The most obvious conclusion drawn from this perspective is that there is no overarching theory of complexity that allows us to ignore the contingent aspects of complex systems. If something is really complex, it cannot be adequately described by means of a simple theory. Engaging with complexity entails engaging with specific complex systems. Despite this we can, at a very basic level, make general remarks concerning the conditions for complex behaviour and the dynamics of complex systems. Furthermore, I suggest that complex systems can be modelled. The models could be computationally implemented, and may lead to machines that can perform more complex tasks. The models themselves, however, will have to be at least as complex as the systems they model, and may therefore not result in any simplification of our understanding of the system itself. As an example of such models, I make extensive use of neural networks – an approach also known as connectionism. As a matter of fact, the significance of postmodern theory for the study of complexity is underscored by arguing that there are structural similarities between the operation of neural networks and Derrida's descriptions of the working of language.

Apart from introductory chapters on connectionism (Chapter 2) and post-structuralism (Chapter 3), and a dismissal of Searle's contributions to the debate (Chapter 4), the central issues discussed are representation (Chapter 5) and self-organisation (Chapter 6). A discussion, or perhaps a deconstruction, of the notion of representation exemplifies the contribution that a primarily philosophical analysis can make to modelling techniques. Conversely, the discussion of self-organisation – a notion usually (but certainly not exclusively) encountered in a scientific context – helps us to make the (philosophical) point that the behaviour of a system without a predetermined or fixed structure is not necessarily random or chaotic, in other words, that anything does not go.

The book does not engage with moral theory in a systematic way, but it is impossible, of course, to operate in a value-free space. Ethical issues therefore do surface now and then, especially in Chapter 7. The characterisation of complexity and complex systems developed in the present book certainly has implications for social and moral theory that demand to be developed further. This, I hope, will be a more central aspect of future projects.

I would like to thank the following people for the contributions they have made towards the development of the ideas presented here: Johan Degenaar, Mary Hesse, Jannie Hofmeyr, and the members of the two interdisciplinary discussion groups at the University of Stellenbosch, one based in the arts faculty, the other in the sciences. The help of Esmarié Smit in the completion of the manuscript was invaluable.

Previous versions of some of the material used in Chapters 2, 3 and 7 have appeared in the *South African Journal of Philosophy*. Permission to rework that material is gratefully acknowledged.

1 Approaching complexity

The worlds of science and philosophy have never existed in isolation, but one could perhaps argue that the relationship between them is entering a new phase. The ubiquitous pressure to do *applied* research certainly has something to do with it, but there is also another, overtly less political, reason: the immense increase in the importance of technology. At first glance one would suspect that this may decrease the importance of the philosophical perspective, that the importance of philosophy is somehow linked to the importance of theory only, but my suggestion is that the contrary is true. Not that theory is unimportant, or that theoretical aspects of science are not philosophical. Few scientific endeavours have been as 'philosophical' as contemporary theoretical physics. The argument is rather that the technologisation of science (as well as the rest of our life-world) is changing the relationship between science and philosophy in a radical way.

Since we are in the midst of this process of change, a clear description of what is happening is not easy, but the heart of the matter is that our technologies have become more powerful than our theories. We are capable of doing things that we do not understand. We can perform gene-splicing without fully understanding how genes interact. We can make pharmaceutics without being able to explain effects and predict side-effects. We can create new sub-atomic particles without knowing precisely whether they actually exist outside of the laboratory. We can store, and retrieve, endless bits of information without knowing what they mean. Central to all these developments are the phenomenal capacities of the electronic computer. It forms part of most of our tools (like washing machines and motor cars); it infiltrates our social world (think of financial matters and entertainment); and it is rapidly becoming the most important medium for communication. Although we know that nothing 'strange' happens inside a computer, nobody can grasp all aspects of what happens when a computer is performing a sophisticated task – at least not down to the level of switching between zeros and ones. It is simply too complex.

The power of technology has opened new possibilities for science. One of the most important scientific tools has always been the analytical method. If something is too complex to be grasped as a whole, it is divided into manageable units which can be analysed separately and then put together again. However, the study of complex dynamic systems has uncovered a fundamental flaw in the analytical method. A complex system is not constituted merely by the sum of its components, but also by the intricate *relationships* between these components. In 'cutting up' a system, the analytical method destroys what it seeks to understand. Fortunately this does not mean that the investigation of complexity is hopeless. Modelling techniques on powerful computers allow us to simulate the behaviour of complex systems without having to understand them. We can do with technology what we cannot do with science. The increased interest in the theory of complexity over the past decade is therefore not surprising.

The rise of powerful technology is not an unconditional blessing. We have to deal with what we do not understand, and that demands new ways of thinking. It is in this sense that I argue that philosophy has an important role to play, not by providing a meta-description of that which happens in science and technology, but by being an integral part of scientific and technological practice. Specific philosophical perspectives can influence the way we approach complex systems, and I want to argue that some of these perspectives – often broadly labelled as postmodern – are of special value to the study of complexity. In order to apply some aspects of postmodern theory to the study of complex systems, a general understanding of what a complex system is should first be developed.

A SKETCH OF COMPLEX SYSTEMS

At this stage it could be expected of one to provide at least a working definition of what 'complexity' might mean. Unfortunately the concept remains elusive at both the qualitative and quantitative levels. One useful description, by Luhmann (1985: 25), states that complexity entails that, in a system, there are more possibilities than can be actualised. This can hardly serve as definition, but perhaps one should not be surprised if complexity cannot be given a simple definition. Instead, an analysis of characteristics of complex systems can be attempted in order to develop a general description that is not constrained by a specific, *a priori* definition. That is what will be attempted in this section. I will turn to the problem of quantifying complexity in the next section.

Before turning to some characteristics of complex systems, we have to look at two important distinctions. The distinction between 'simple' and 'complex' is not as sharp as we may intuitively think (Nicolis and Prigogine 1989: 5). Many systems appear simple, but reveal remarkable complexity when examined closely (e.g. a leaf). Others appear complex, but can be described simply, e.g. some machines, such as the internal combustion engine. To compound matters, complexity is not located at a specific, identifiable site in a system. Because complexity results from the interaction between the components of a system, complexity is manifested at the level of the system itself. There is neither something at a level below (a source), nor at a level above (a meta-description), capable of capturing the essence of complexity. The distinction between complex and simple often becomes a function of our 'distance' from the system (Serra and Zanarini 1990: 4, 5), i.e. of the kind of description of the system we are using. A little aquarium can be quite simple as a decoration (seen from afar), but as a *system* it can be quite complex (seen from close by). This does not imply that complexity is merely a linguistic phenomenon, or *simply* a function of our description of the system. Complex systems do have characteristics that are not merely determined by the point of view of the observer. It does, however, imply that care has to be taken when talking about complexity. The simple and the complex often mask each other.

A second important distinction, and one that is equally difficult to maintain consistently, is the one between complex and complicated. Some systems have a very large number of components and perform sophisticated tasks, but in a way that can be analysed (in the full sense of the word) accurately. Such a system is complicated. Other systems are constituted by such intricate sets of non-linear relationships and feedback loops that only certain aspects of them can be analysed at a time. Moreover, these analyses would always cause distortions. Systems of this kind are complex. I have heard it said (by someone from France, of course) that a jumbo jet is complicated, but that a mayonnaise is complex. Other examples of complicated systems, systems that can, in principle, be given an exact description, would be a CD-player, a snowflake, the Mandelbrot set. Complex systems are usually associated with living things: a bacterium, the brain, social systems, language. This distinction remains an analytical one that is undermined specifically by powerful new technologies (e.g. is a fast computer with a very large memory complex or complicated?), but it is useful in developing a description of the characteristics of complex systems. I offer the following list:[1]

(i)   Complex systems consist of a large number of elements. When the number is relatively small, the behaviour of the elements can often be given a formal description in conventional terms. However, when the number becomes sufficiently large, conventional means (e.g. a system of differential equations) not only become impractical, they also cease to assist in any *understanding* of the system.

(ii)   A large number of elements are necessary, but not sufficient. The grains of sand on a beach do not interest us as a complex system. In order to constitute a complex system, the elements have to interact, and this interaction must be dynamic. A complex system changes with time. The interactions do not have to be *physical*; they can also be thought of as the transference of *information*.

(iii)   The interaction is fairly rich, i.e. any element in the system influences, and is influenced by, quite a few other ones. The behaviour of the system, however, is not determined by the exact amount of interactions associated with specific elements. If there are enough elements in the system (of which some are redundant), a number of sparsely connected elements can perform the same function as that of one richly connected element.

(iv)   The interactions themselves have a number of important characteristics. Firstly, the interactions are *non-linear*. A large system of linear elements can usually be collapsed into an equivalent system that is very much smaller. Non-linearity also guarantees that small causes can have large results, and vice versa. It is a precondition for complexity.

(v)   The interactions usually have a fairly short range, i.e. information is received primarily from immediate neighbours. Long-range interaction is not impossible, but practical constraints usually force this consideration. This does not preclude wide-ranging *influence* – since the interaction is rich, the route from one element to any other can usually be covered in a few steps. As a result, the influence gets modulated along the way. It can be enhanced, suppressed or altered in a number of ways.

(vi)   There are loops in the interactions. The effect of any activity can feed back onto itself, sometimes directly, sometimes after a number of intervening stages. This feedback can be positive (enhancing, stimulating) or negative (detracting, inhibiting). Both kinds are necessary. The technical term for this aspect of a complex system is *recurrency*.

(vii) Complex systems are usually open systems, i.e. they interact with their environment. As a matter of fact, it is often difficult to define the border of a complex system. Instead of being a characteristic of the system itself, the scope of the system is usually determined by the purpose of the *description* of the system, and is thus often influenced by the position of the observer. This process is called *framing*. Closed systems are usually merely complicated.

(viii) Complex systems operate under conditions far from equilibrium. There has to be a constant flow of energy to maintain the organisation of the system and to ensure its survival. Equilibrium is another word for death.

(ix)   Complex systems have a history. Not only do they evolve through time, but their past is co-responsible for their present behaviour. Any analysis of a complex system that ignores the dimension of time is incomplete, or at most a synchronic snapshot of a diachronic process.

(x)   Each element in the system is ignorant of the behaviour of the system as a whole, it responds only to information that is available to it locally. This point is vitally important. If each element 'knew' what was happening to the system as a whole, all of the complexity would have to be present *in that element*. This would either entail a physical impossibility in the sense that a single element does not have the necessary capacity, or constitute a metaphysical move in the sense that 'consciousness' of the whole is contained in one particular unit. Complexity is the result of a rich interaction of simple elements that only respond to the limited information each of them are presented with. When we look at the behaviour of a complex system as a whole, our focus shifts from the individual element in the system to the complex *structure* of the system. The complexity emerges as a result of the patterns of interaction between the elements.[2]

Let us illustrate these characteristics through some examples. Consider a snowflake. From a distance it appears to be a pretty simple object, but when we examine it closer it reveals remarkable detail. The snowflake is arranged hexagonally with each of the six 'branches' showing an elaborate and beautifully patterned structure. Although all snowflakes share this form, every specific one is different. A snowflake consists of a large amount of elements (water molecules) interacting through its crystalline structure. Each molecule is influenced only by local information (there is no external decision as to what the position of the molecule must be in the snowflake), but the relationships between the molecules are fairly fixed. There are no real feedback loops and there is no evolution (except perhaps decay). As far as its structure is concerned, it is not really an open system. It is in temporary equilibrium, cannot adapt to its environment, and therefore quickly loses its structure. A snowflake, although wondrously complex in appearance, is only complicated.

Let us then examine some truly complex systems. The human brain is considered by many to be the most complex object known. Similarly, the language with which we communicate daily does not yield to analytical descriptions. These two complex systems – the brain and natural language – will receive detailed attention throughout this study. I will therefore elucidate the ten characteristics of a complex system using another example: the economic system.[3]

In order to frame our description, we have to decide what our 'distance' from the system will be: in other words, what level of detail are we going to consider? If we stand far away, we could only consider the activity of large financial institutions – banks, large corporations, even countries. Obviously a lot of smaller detail will get lost in the process. If we are going to examine the system in microscopic detail, we may have to keep track of the status of every individual penny. In that case we will run the risk of all meaningful patterns being obscured by the buzzing activity at the lower level.[4] Let us, for argument's sake, frame the system in a way that will allow us to consider individual human beings – in their capacity as economic agents – as the elements of our complex system, and to draw the border of the system around a single country. The ten characteristics of complex systems will then manifest themselves in the following way:

(i)   The economically active people in a country certainly comprise a large amount of elements, usually several million.

(ii)   The various individuals interact by lending, borrowing, investing and exchanging money for goods. These relationships change continually.

(iii)   An economic agent interacts with a large number of the other elements: shops, banks, other agents. Some agents are more active than others, but this is not a function of the amount of money they transfer, or indicative of their influence on the system.

(iv)   The interaction is non-linear: money can receive compounded interest; small investments can produce large returns (e.g. buying the right shares at the right time, or vice versa).

(v)   Economic agents primarily interact with others that are in their near vicinity (not necessarily in a spatial sense): local shops or providers of service, as well as their colleagues or partners. They can, however, easily interact with more distant parties via intermediaries like banks or brokers.

(vi)   The activity of an agent may eventually reflect back on itself. A good investment can produce good returns (positive feedback), and overspending can result in a shortage in the money supply (negative feedback). Without feedback there would be no economic system – who would invest if there were no returns? Activities can also reflect back after a large number of intermediary steps. The complexities of inflation serve as a good example.

(vii)   The economic system is certainly open. It is virtually impossible to draw its borders. It is continuously influenced by the political system, agriculture (and therefore the climatic conditions), science and technology, international relationships, the stability of the society, etc. There is a constant flow of commodities, products, money and information through the system.

(viii) Since the economic system is driven by the dynamics of supply and demand it can never be in a state of equilibrium. It may be growing or shrinking, swing up or down; it never stands still, not even in a recession. Even when we refer to a 'stable' economy, the 'stability' has to be understood in dynamic terms.

(ix)   Economic systems are greatly influenced by their history. Today's prices largely depend on yesterday's. Many important economic trends change fairly slowly over long periods of time, but specific influences can cause sharp changes.

(x)   An economic agent can only act on the available information. It does not know what all the other agents are doing. When, for example, an agent wants to purchase a commodity, a decision is based on a number of 'local' factors: how much do I want it?, can I afford it?, in place of what else will it be purchased?, etc. The effects of this act on the inflation rate, the balance of payments, investor's confidence, interest rates, and the like, are not normally taken into account, even though this act does affect (minutely, but no less than other similar acts) all these factors.

Our description of the economic system may seem a little thin (which in many respects it is), but there are good reasons for this. We have been describing the elements of the system and their interactions on the level at which they operate. If we want to shift the discussion to more complex economic phenomena (gross national product, stock-market indexes, the gold price, etc.), nothing extra needs to be added; the phenomena mentioned emerge as a result of nothing more than the interactions between the various elements of the system. These interactions often take the form of clusters of elements which co-operate with each other, and also compete with other clusters. A bank, for example, is nothing more than a number of individuals grouped together to perform specific functions. The components of the complex economic system do not consist of different *types* of things (banks, the state, corporations *and* individuals); they consists of individual agents clustered together to form the larger-scale phenomena. The higher-order complexities of which we hope to get an understanding reside not in any of the individual agents, but in the rich pattern of interactions between them.

The example of the economic system allows us to make a last significant point. An element in the system may belong to more than one clustering. A person may bank with more than one bank, work for a big corporation and play the stock-market on his own. Clusters should not be interpreted in a spatial sense, or seen as fixed, hermetically sealed entities. They can grow or shrink, be subdivided or absorbed, flourish or decay. The clusters are dynamic and interact with other clusters, both directly as well as through the individual members they share with each other.

The ten characteristics proposed here help us to talk about complexity in a qualitative way, but do not provide us with a method to *measure* complexity. We would like to be able to deal with complexity in a more quantitative way, especially when modelling complex systems. To what extent is this possible?

QUANTIFYING COMPLEXITY

One of the first successful attempts to deal with complex phenomena was the development of thermodynamics in the second half of the nineteenth century, particularly in the work of Ludwig Boltzmann.[5] Through the formulation of three 'laws' it allowed scientists to deal with the use and transfer of energy in an accurate way, without getting entangled in the low-level complexities.

... equilibrium thermodynamics was the first response of physics to the problem of nature's complexity. This response was expressed in terms of the dissipation of energy, the forgetting of initial conditions, and evolution toward disorder. Classical dynamics, the science of eternal, reversible trajectories, was alien to the problems facing the nineteenth century, which was dominated by the concept of evolution. Equilibrium thermodynamics was in a position to oppose its view of time to that of other sciences: for thermodynamics, time implies degradation and death.

(Prigogine and Stengers 1984: 129)

In classical mechanics, time was reversible, and therefore not part of the equation. In thermodynamics time plays a vital role. This is perhaps best expressed in the second law of thermodynamics, which states that the entropy of a system can only increase. Entropy can be seen as a measure of the 'disorder' in a system. As a system transforms energy, less and less of it remains in a usable form, and the 'disorder' in the system increases.

The concept of entropy is a complex one, and it was a stroke of genius by Claude Shannon to use it as a measure for the information content of a message. In two seminal papers (Shannon 1948, 1949) he developed a mathematical theory of communication which formed the basis for modern information theory. By replacing 'energy' with 'information' in the equations of thermodynamics, he could show that the amount of information in a message is equal to its 'entropy'. The more disorderly a message, the higher is its information content. An example will clarify the argument. Consider a message consisting of a string of digits that is being transmitted to you one at a time. If, for example, the string consists of threes only, you will notice this quickly at the receiving end. The next digit is so predictable that it will carry no new information. Although the message is highly structured, its information content is very low. The sequence 1489 1489 1489 has a slightly higher information content, but also becomes predictable very quickly. The less able the receiver is to predict the next digit in the sequence, the higher the information content of the message. A message high in information is one low in predictable structure, and therefore high in 'entropy'.

Because Shannon's theory was neatly formalised, it was possible to apply it to many engineering problems with ease. Communications technology in particular benefited tremendously, and there is no denying the practical importance of his work. The entropy theory of information does, however, have a problematic implication: if information equals entropy, then the message with the highest information content is one that is completely random. Obviously there is some tension between the concepts of 'information' and 'randomness'. Despite the elegance of the entropy theory, there is reason to claim that it is not an adequate model for the understanding of complex systems like human cognition (see Katz and Dorfman 1992: 167), where the intricate structure certainly cannot be equated with 'randomness'.

Some interesting new perspectives are supplied by the work of Gregory Chaitin (1975, 1987). In his reinterpretation of information theory, in what he has termed 'algorithmic information theory', randomness is defined not in terms of unpredictability, but in terms of 'incompressibility'. His definition of randomness is the following: 'A series of numbers is random if the smallest algorithm capable of specifying it to a computer has about the same number of bits of information as the series itself' (Chaitin 1975: 48).[6] Consider a sequence of numbers of significant length, say a thousand. If this sequence consists of threes only, it is clearly possible to write a very simple computer program to generate it. Something like:

Step 1. Print '3'.
Step 2. Repeat step 1 a thousand times.

This program is clearly very much shorter than the original sequence, which therefore has a very low level of randomness. As the sequence of numbers becomes more complex(!), the length of the program necessary to produce it becomes longer. When the program becomes as long as the sequence, the sequence is said to be random.

For a given sequence, there can obviously be a large number of programs, some of which can be quite elaborate and lengthy. We are only concerned with the shortest or smallest program capable of performing the task. Such programs are called minimal programs (Chaitin 1975: 49). Note that the minimal program is itself random by definition, irrespective of whether the series it generates is random or not, since it cannot be compressed any further. It is therefore possible to reduce any non-random sequence to a random one (remember that the program is – number-theoretically – only a sequence of numbers), with the random one being shorter.

Through this process, randomness becomes a measure for the amount of information in a sequence, but, and this is vital, randomness understood no longer in terms of unpredictability, but in terms of the denseness with which the information is packed. It also provides us with an interesting definition of complexity: the complexity of a series is equal to the size of the minimal program necessary to produce that series (Chaitin 1975: 49).[7]

In a certain sense we have taken a long route to arrive at a truism: complexity is complex. A complex system cannot be reduced to a simple one if it wasn't simple (or perhaps merely complicated) to start off with. This claim has implications for an ideal many scientists have: to find the basic principles that govern all of nature. The success of the analytical method has created the illusion that all phenomena are governed by a set of laws or rules that could be made explicit. The mercenary use of Occam's razor, often early in an investigation, is an indication of this belief. Chaitin's analyses help us to realise that truly complex problems can only be approached with complex resources. This realisation is also a reinterpretation of the anti-reductionist position. It does not deny that complex systems are built out of normal, material components. It does, however, deny that a description of these components *and their interactions*, explaining the behaviour of the system as a whole, is practically possible. A complex system cannot be reduced to a collection of its basic constituents, not because the system is not constituted by them, but because too much of the relational information gets lost in the process.

Some final remarks concerning Chaitin's definition of complexity: Chaitin works in the context of numerical formal systems, albeit at a very low level. Such formal systems, I will argue below, provide an inadequate starting-point for modelling complexity in general. His analyses would, strictly speaking, be applicable mostly to complicated phenomena. On an intuitive level, however, the notion of 'incompressibility' remains very fruitful. It reminds us that when dealing with complexity, there are no short-cuts without peril. The notion should nevertheless not be used absolutely. The complex systems we are interested in are never completely 'minimal'; they contain a lot of spare capacity or redundancy. This is necessary for more than one reason: it provides robustness, space for development and the means for plasticity. A clearer picture of why some 'free space' is necessary will emerge in the next section when we examine two important aspects of complex systems which our models have to capture. For now we can conclude that a strict measure for complexity does not seem feasible. To describe a complex system you have, in a certain sense, to *repeat* the system.

TWO INDISPENSABLE CAPABILITIES OF COMPLEX SYSTEMS

Complex systems have to grapple with a changing environment. Depending on the severity of these changes, great demands can be made on the resources of the system. To cope with these demands the system must have two capabilities: it must be able to store information concerning the environment for future use; and it must be able to adapt its structure when necessary. The first of these will be discussed as the process of *representation*; the second, which concerns the development and change of internal structure without the *a priori* necessity of an external designer, as the process of *self-organisation*.

These capabilities are vital and will each receive detailed attention in separate chapters. In this section they will only be introduced in broad terms. It is important, however, to realise the implications of these capabilities for our *models* of complex systems. Any model of a truly complex system will have to possess these capabilities. In other words, the processes of representation and self-organisation must be simulated by the model. This implies that these two capabilities will have to be given some kind of formal description. I will argue that this is possible.

Representing information

In order to respond appropriately to its environment, a complex system must be able to gather information about that environment and store it for future use. Formulated differently, the structure of the system cannot consist of a random collection of elements; they must have some *meaning*. In traditional philosophical terms, this means that the system must somehow 'represent' the information important to its existence.

The search to find mechanisms for this process of representation constitutes a set of long-standing philosophical problems. How does the brain represent the world? What is the relationship between linguistic components and the objects they describe? When is a theory an adequate description of the phenomena it tries to explain? Solutions to these questions have been suggested, but they usually postulate a one-to-one correspondence between elements of the system and specific external causes. This atomistic approach is the legacy of the analytical method and usually takes the form of splitting the structure of the system, and the meaning of that structure, into separate levels. For example, in language, a distinction is made between the structure of language (its syntax), and the meaning of the syntactic units (its semantics). These two levels are usually taken to be independent of each other. The syntactic level is seen as a specific implementation of the semantic level. A concept can be 'implemented' either in Spanish or in Japanese, but it would retain its essential meaning. Similarly, an object in the world can be represented either in the brain or in a computer – the implementation is different but the representation is the same.

I will argue that this understanding of representation is not adequate when describing a complex system. Meaning is conferred not by a one-to-one correspondence of a symbol with some external concept or object, but by the relationships between the structural components of the system itself. This does not deny a causal relationship between the outside and inside of the system. It does, however, deny that the structure of the system is *determined* by the outside. Meaning is the result of a process, and this process is dialectical – involving elements from inside and outside – as well as historical, in the sense that previous states of the system are vitally important. The process takes place in an active, open and complex system.

In the section devoted to the problem of representation (Chapter 5) I will argue for the notion of 'distributed representation'. In such a framework the elements of the system have no representational meaning by themselves, but only in terms of patterns of relationships with many other elements. Furthermore, the abstract level of meaning (the 'semantic' level) becomes redundant, or, rather, unnecessary, for the process of modelling the system. Distributed representation is best implemented in connectionist (or neural) networks, and I will argue that these networks provide appropriate models for complex systems. Before these models are described in more detail, and compared with the traditional approach, something must be said about the other capability of complex systems, i.e. the way in which they develop organised structure.

Self-organisation

A complex system, such as a living organism or a growing economy, has to develop its structure and be able to adapt that structure in order to cope with changes in the environment. Claiming an external designer (or Designer) merely begs the question of the origin of complexity, and we have to find mechanisms by which a system can acquire and adapt its internal structure on an evolutionary basis.

The key concept here is the notion of self-organisation. This does not imply that a complex system contains some form of internal 'subject' that controls the behaviour of the system; as a matter of fact, the whole notion of central control becomes suspect. What will be described in the section on self-organisation (Chapter 6) is a process whereby a system can develop a complex structure from fairly unstructured beginnings. This process changes the relationships between the distributed elements of the system under influence of both the external environment and the history of the system. Since the system has to cope with unpredictable changes in the environment, the development of the structure cannot be contained in a rigid programme that controls the behaviour of the system. The system must be 'plastic'. It will also be shown that the process of self-organisation can be modelled mathematically. The notion of 'autopoiesis', like the notion of 'emergence', does not involve anything mystical.

The general description of complex systems will be influenced by models of complexity. Such models must share the characteristics of the systems they model. We will now examine two possible types of models.

MODELLING COMPLEX SYSTEMS: TWO APPROACHES

Two perspectives on models

Why would we want to model complexity? We can answer from two perspectives. From the traditional scientific perspective, models are required in order to predict and control the behaviour of complex systems. The advantages are obvious. Better models can give scientists a much firmer grasp on the complexities encountered in economics, biology, medicine, psychology, sociology, law and politics, to name but a few. We can only benefit from better theories explaining disease, mental illness, crime and the vagaries of the economic system. To be effective, however, these models have to work, they have to produce results. At this point, however, there are problems. How are these models to be tested and evaluated? How accurate should they be? How much detail has to be considered? By and large, specific scientific models of complexity have severe limitations. The most successful are those whose limitations are explicitly visible; models that remain within the constraints determined by a specific modelling process. Examples here would include models of flow-dynamics and turbulence, statistical quantum mechanics and, in computer science, well-designed expert systems and signal-processing systems.

From a more general philosophical perspective we can say that we wish to model complex systems because we want to *understand* them better. The main requirement for our models accordingly shifts from having to be correct to being rich in information. This does not mean that the relationship between the model and the system itself becomes less important, but the shift from control and prediction to understanding does have an effect on our approach to complexity: the evaluation of our models in terms of *performance* can be deferred. Once we have a better understanding of the dynamics of complexity, we can start looking for the similarities and differences between different complex systems and thereby develop a clearer understanding of the strengths and limitations of different models. This kind of perspective also allows us to speculate more, and to incorporate ideas that would not be permissible from a strictly scientific perspective.

One of the aims of this study will be to show that in order to model complexity, we will need both the scientific and the philosophical perspectives. To paraphrase a little, one can say that science without philosophy is blind, and philosophy without science is paralysed. Co-operation between them will benefit both. On the one hand, models of complexity will only become successful in scientific practice once we begin to understand more about the nature of complexity. On the other hand, our understanding will only improve if we actually test our models scientifically. An interdisciplinary approach can therefore open up new avenues for research. It can, for example, be shown that certain models of language (from the traditionally philosophical domain) are equivalent to certain models of the brain, usually considered to be the domain of the natural sciences (see Cilliers 1990). As our exploration of complexity continues, the implications of discoveries made in one field for knowledge in another field will be emphasised.

In the remainder of this section I will discuss two possible answers to the question '*How* would we model complexity?' Both approaches can be modelled in scientific terms and both have their own philosophical allegiances.

Rule-based symbol systems

Over the past forty years the search for artificial intelligence (AI) has provided the focal point for research on models of complexity. The rapidly growing capabilities of the digital computer created the expectation that it would be possible to construct computers capable of behaving intelligently. Just how intelligent these might be (sub- or superhuman) depended on your belief in the power of the methods and tools of AI. Generally speaking, the early stages of this research (up to the early sixties) were marked by a great deal of optimism. Soon there were computers solving mathematical problems and playing chess, but the important hallmarks of intelligence – perception, movement and the use of language – proved to be complex beyond all estimation. In these respects no computing device has capabilities even remotely close to those of human beings.

Although the expectations of what AI can achieve have been deflated somewhat (and the required time-scales inflated), it is incorrect to declare the program a failure. Along the way a number of quite useful by-products were produced. One example would be expert systems. These systems model the knowledge of some 'expert' on a specific domain of knowledge (like geological surveying or the diagnosis of cervical cancer) as a set of rules on a computer. A non-expert can then use this system to perform some tasks within the specified domain. Although expert systems deal with some aspects of complexity and intelligence, they are notoriously inflexible. Arguments attempting explanations for the shortcomings of the AI paradigm will be provided throughout this study; first, however, we need a description of the basic characteristics of a formal symbol system.

A formal system consists of a number of tokens or symbols, like pieces in a game. These symbols can be combined into patterns by means of a set of rules which defines what is or is not permissible (e.g. the rules of chess). These rules are strictly formal, i.e. they conform to a precise logic. The configuration of the symbols at any specific moment constitutes a 'state' of the system. A specific state will activate the applicable rules which then transform the system from one state to another. If the set of rules governing the behaviour of the system are exact and complete, one could test whether various possible states of the system are or are not permissible.[8]

We now have a set of symbols that can have certain configurations. The next step is to make these symbols 'represent' something. For example, if each of the symbols stands for a word in a language, then the rules of the system (the grammar) will determine the various combinations of words that can be made in that (formal) language. The permissible states of the system then translate into valid sentences of that language.[9] The interpretation of the symbols, also known as the 'semantics' of the system, is independent of the rules governing the system. One and the same semantic level can therefore be implemented in different *actual* formal systems, provided that these systems can be shown to be equivalent to each other on a logical level.

Formal systems can be quite simple, e.g. the pieces and rules necessary to play noughts and crosses (tic-tac-toe), or extremely complicated, e.g. a modern digital computer. The range of things that can be done on a computer gives us an indication of the power of formal systems. This range is so bewildering that we often forget that it is a formal system, consisting only of a set of tokens manipulated by rules (in this case called a program). The formal aspects of computing devices are best described by turning to the abstract models of automatic formal systems, known as Turing machines. From these mathematical models both the generality and power of computers become clear. One can also show the equivalence between different types of Turing machines and different formal languages, e.g. those used by Chomsky (1957) to model language.

Symbolic rule-based systems constitute the classical approach to the modelling of complexity. The behaviour of the complex system has to be reduced to a set of rules that describes the system adequately. The problem lies in finding those rules, assuming that they exist. Can a system like natural language or the human brain really be reduced to a set of rules? Classical AI claims that it can. Before turning to another approach, let me summarise the main characteristics of rule-based systems (following Serra and Zanarini 1990: 26):

- Rule-based symbol systems model complex systems on an *abstract* (semantic) level. The symbols are used to represent important concepts directly. In this way a lot of the contingent aspects of the complex systems, i.e. the unnecessary detail of the implementation, can be ignored. The model consists of the set of logical relationships between the symbols (the production rules).
- The set of rules are governed by a system of *centralised control*, known as the meta-rules of the system. This control system decides which of the production rules should become active at every stage of the computation. If the central control fails, the whole system fails.
- Each concept has a symbol dedicated to it, or, conversely, each symbol *represents* a specific concept. This is known as local representation. A theory of representation is central to formal explanations of mind and language, as can be seen in the Chomsky/Fodor model, for example.

What has been summarised here is a general method often employed in AI research. This method is obviously not the only one. Researchers differ on many points of detail and not everybody claims the same scope and power for rule-based systems. In general there is a split between the supporters of strong AI, who claim that formal systems provide an adequate model for all aspects of human intelligence, and the supporters of weak AI, who merely see formal systems as a powerful tool. Some of these internal tensions will come to light in Chapter 4 when we analyse John Searle's arguments against strong AI. This case-study will also further elucidate the use of formal systems as models for the brain and language. My dismissal of rule-based systems as an adequate model for complex systems will rely on my critique of local representation (in Chapter 5).

Connectionist models

In discussions of complexity, the human brain has always held a special place, not only because of its own structural complexity, but also because of its capability to deal with complexity. For instance, how does the brain perform complex tasks like the use of language or playing the violin? It is to be expected that questions of this kind would prompt efforts to model the brain itself.

Questions like these certainly prompted the young Sigmund Freud to construct a rather fascinating model of the brain in 1895 (Freud 1950). This model not only underpinned most of his later themes, but it has also been argued that it is compatible with most of modern neurology (Pribram and Gill 1976). Modelling the brain advanced another step when McCulloch and Pitts (1943) developed mathematical models of neurons and showed how combinations of neurons could perform calculations. These models triggered strong research efforts and in the late fifties Frank Rosenblatt (1958) achieved considerable success with his so-called 'perceptron' models. These models still had a number of limitations which were ruthlessly pointed out by Minsky and Papert (1969). Their book resulted in a shift from neural-inspired models to formal symbol systems. Neural models only regained their lost ground in the early eighties after mathematical methods were found to overcome the limitations of perceptrons. Since then these models have received unprecedented attention in a wide range of applications (Rumelhart and McClelland 1986).

In this section I will introduce neurally inspired 'computational' models, variously known as neural networks, distributed processors or connectionist models. Detailed discussions of their characteristics, use and philosophical implications will follow in the rest of this study. A brief introduction to how they work will be given in Chapter 2.

From a strictly functional point of view, the brain consists of nothing more than a huge network of richly interconnected neurons. Each neuron can be seen as a simple processor that calculates the sum of all its inputs, and, should this sum exceed a certain threshold, it generates an output. This in turn becomes the input to all the neurons that are connected to the present one. Each connection is mediated by a synapse. The synapse can cause the incoming signal to either excite or inhibit the target neuron and it also determines the strength of the influence. Incoming information from a sensory organ, for instance, is processed in this way and distributed to other parts of the brain where it can have specific effects, e.g. the moving of a muscle.[10]

This level of the brain's operation can be modelled by means of a network of interconnected nodes. Each node takes the sum of its inputs and generates an output. The output is determined by the transfer function of the node, which has to be non-linear. The connection ('synapse') between any two nodes has a certain 'weight', which can be positive or negative and which determines the strength of the influence of node A on node B. In any specific connection, the information flows in only one direction, but nothing prevents two connections between A and B – one from A to B and one from B to A. Any node can also be connected to itself, either directly, or via other nodes.

How does such a network process information? If certain nodes are taken as input nodes, i.e. nodes that receive information from outside the network, and certain nodes are taken as output nodes, the network can 'process' the input and generate an output. The value of the output is determined by two things: the input values and the present values of the weights in the network. For example, the inputs can come from a 'retina' of light-sensitive sensors and the output of the network can be connected to a lamp. With the right set of weights in the network, this system can sense whether it is dark or light and accordingly make the lamp brighter or weaker. The same network, with different weights (and sensors), could perform a variety of other tasks, including the recognition of changes and trends.

It should be clear now that the characteristics of the network are determined by the weights. The vital question is the following: where do the different values of the weights come from? They could of course be set by an external agent, like the programmer of a formal system, but we wish to find a model of a system that does not need a designer, a model of a system that can self-organise. Suggestions for such a mechanism have been made in remarkable detail by Freud in his model of the brain (see Cilliers 1990), but as far as the connectionist models we know today are concerned, the use-principle formulated by Donald Hebb (1949) provided the clue.

Hebb suggested that the connection strength between two neurons should increase proportionally to how often it is used. Consider three neurons, A, B and C. Each time both A and B are active simultaneously, the strength of their interconnection (let us call it W_{ab}) should be increased slightly, but when they are not active, W_{ab} should decay slowly. In this way, if A and B are often active together W_{ab} will grow, but if A and B are only associated spuriously and A and C more regularly, W_{ab} will decay and W_{ac} will grow. In this way, a network will develop internal structure, based only on the local information available at each neuron. This development of structure can also be called 'learning'.

To clarify the working of Hebb's rule – as it has become known – let us return to our example of a network that has to switch on a lamp when it gets dark. Initially the network is untrained, i.e. the weights in the network have random values and it cannot perform the tasks. In order to train the network the lamp has to be switched on (by an external agent) every time it gets dark. When the lamp is on, the output neurons of the network will be forced into activity, and this will be automatically associated with the corresponding input, or absence of input, to the network. As soon as it becomes light, the lamp is switched off and the network now has to associate a different output condition with a different set of input values. If this cycle is repeated a number of times, the network will adjust its internal weights, without external intervention. Through the application of Hebb's rule at each neuron, the input conditions representing darkness are associated with an active output, and vice versa for conditions of light. After it has been trained, the network will be able to perform the required task by itself. Exactly the same principle can be used to 'teach' the network completely different tasks, e.g. to turn on a tap when the earth is dry, or to recognise someone's voice.

Hebb's rule, formulated in this way, appears to be only a qualitative principle, but it has been given a mathematical formulation by several authors (e.g. Grossberg 1982, 1988). The main problem that hampered the development of neural network models was the absence of a mathematical model for adjusting the weights of neurons situated somewhere in the middle of the network, and not directly connected to the input or output. The problem was solved by a few independent researchers during the seventies – the best-known formulation being the so-called 'generalised delta rule' (Rumelhart and McClelland 1986, Vol. 1: 318–362). The rule is used in the popular 'back-propagation' method for training feedforward neural networks (discussed in more detail in Chapter 2).

We can summarise this introductory description on connectionist models as follows. A network of interconnected neurons (which can be modelled mathematically) can learn to perform complex tasks either by showing it examples of these tasks successfully performed, or by using criteria internal to the network that indicates success. These tasks include pattern recognition, motor control, information-processing, regulation, prediction and replication. The only requirement is that there should be some 'sensor' to get the information into the network, and some 'motor' that allows the output to have an external effect. Inside the network itself there are only neurons adjusting their weights based on the local information available to them. At the level of the individual neuron no complex behaviour is discernible, but the *system* of neurons is capable of performing specific, complex tasks. Complex behaviour emerges from the interaction between many simple processors that respond in a non-linear fashion to local information.

COMPARING RULE-BASED AND CONNECTIONIST MODELS

Both the approaches to complexity mentioned in the previous section have strong support. The rule-based approach has been adopted by AI researchers, computational linguists in the Chomskian tradition, and cognitive scientists – especially those who adhere to a representational theory of mind (Fodor 1975, 1981; Sterelny 1990). Connectionism is supported by a less well-defined, more interdisciplinary group of neuroscientists, psychologists and engineers. Several attempts have been made to dismiss connectionism as simply wrong (e.g. Fodor and Pylyshyn 1988),[11] or to assimilate it (Lloyd 1989), or parts of it (Sterelny 1990), into the rule-based paradigm. I do not deny that there are areas of overlap or that practical models of complexity may combine aspects of both paradigms. However, for the sake of understanding the two approaches properly, we must initially focus on the differences between them. Most of the following differences are important enough to make a persuasive case against the assimilation of connectionism into the rule-based paradigm:[12]

- Whereas formal systems apply inference rules to *logical* variables, neural networks apply evolutive principles to *numerical* variables. Instead of *calculating* a solution, the network *settles* into a condition that satisfies the constraints imposed on it.
- Neural nets have no central control in the classical sense. Processing is distributed over the network and the roles of the various components (or groups of components) change dynamically. This does not preclude any part of the network from developing a regulating function, but that will be determined by the evolutionary needs of the system.
- Every symbol in a rule-based system has a precise, predefined meaning – this constitutes a local representation. In a connectionist network individual neurons have no pre-defined meaning. Changing patterns of activity over several nodes perform meaningful functions. This is often referred to as distributed representation.
- Formal systems have well-defined terminating conditions and results are only produced when these conditions are reached. Connectionist systems tend to dynamically converge on a solution, usually in an asymptotic fashion. The process does not have to terminate; as a matter of fact, usually it will not arrive at a single, final conclusion.
- The internal structure of a connectionist network develops through a process of self-organisation, whereas rule-based systems have to search through pre-programmed options that define the structure largely in an *a priori* fashion. In this sense, learning is an implicit characteristic of neural networks. In rule-based systems, learning can only take place through explicitly formulated procedures.
- Apart from the fact that formal rule-based models have to be interpreted on a semantic level, the model itself is divided into two levels: that of the symbols and that of the rules; or the data and the program. In connectionist models there is only one level, that of the neurons and their weights. Instead of an 'active' program and 'passive' data, you have numerical weights that are dynamically adjusted through interaction. Instead of a program you have memory.

For those accustomed to the high level of abstraction and the crispness of logical inference, the connectionist approach often appears vague, shallow and too sparse. As a result, they have serious misgivings about the approach. Here, in the words of Kolen and Goel (1991), are three such misgivings:

- Connectionist networks cannot represent ' . . . higher order relations. This representational poverty leads to an incapacity for generalisation to higher order relations since a network can only learn what it can represent' (365).
- Connectionist learning methods are 'weak' since they do not make use of external or *a priori* knowledge about the domain being modelled. Domain knowledge has to be 'hard-wired' into the network by a designer.
- 'Connectionist methods for learning do not reflect the structure of the task they address' (369). The same learning method can be used to solve very different tasks.

The first objection merely states a commitment to a strong theory of representation. It is true that networks do not 'represent higher order relations', but that is only a problem if representation is insisted upon. This commitment is made explicitly by Chandrasekaran *et al.* (1988). For them there is an abstract level of 'information-processing' which is higher than any specific realisation thereof, whether that realisation be symbolic or connectionist (30). It is at this abstract level that the 'explanatory power' resides (33). Like Fodor and Pylyshyn (1988) and Lloyd (1989), they claim that connectionists remain committed to representation, and the fact that this representation is 'distributed' makes no difference to anything. I will argue in detail (in Chapter 5) that distributed representation makes all the difference; that, in fact, it undermines the whole concept of representation. The fact that connectionist networks 'cannot represent' becomes a distinct advantage.

The second objection reflects the urge of symbolic modellers to reduce the domain to be modelled to a finite number of explicit principles using logical inference. We have already argued that, when dealing with true complexity, this is often not possible. Connectionist models can implement aspects of complexity *without* performing this reduction. That is their strength. The claim that the weight in the network has to be set to specific values by the designer is simply incorrect. In most cases the weights in the network are explicitly randomised before learning commences. One cannot make use of *a priori* domain knowledge because one often does not know which aspects of the domain are relevant. This also largely answers the third objection, i.e. that the connectionist model is too general and does not reflect the 'structure' of the problem. The structure cannot be reflected, precisely because it cannot be made explicit in symbolic terms. The fact that the same network can be taught to perform 'very different' tasks is not a weakness, but rather an indication of the power of this approach.

Serra and Zanarini (1990: 28–29) point to a few further advantages, which can be summed up in the following two points:

- Networks cope naturally with large amounts of data. The distributed nature of the network is in that respect equivalent to a hologram. No separate local representation is necessary for each bit of data. Input data do not have to be 'interpreted' in terms of symbolic relationships either; they can be given to the network in fairly 'raw' form.

- Because networks operate on a basis of constraint satisfaction, they can cope with contradictions. (Rule-based systems are 'brittle' by nature and become completely unreliable when given contradictory information.) This does not mean that a network can produce 'correct' answers from 'incorrect' data, but it does not blow up, as a logical rule-based system will.[13] A network will either resolve the conflict by giving more weight to other constraints or it will produce no meaningful results. This is an indication of the robustness of the connectionist approach.

As a final recourse, the supporter of formal symbol systems can claim that nothing prevents her/him from continuously adding *ad hoc* rules to her/ his system until it can perform the required task. This may be quite possible, but when dealing with complexity, the demands such an approach will make in terms of time and resources could be astronomical. Furthermore, the more *ad hoc* rules there are, the more 'distributed' the model becomes. To get a working model following this route may end up being nothing else than an extremely tedious way of constructing a connectionist model.

From a slightly more philosophical perspective, Clark and Lutz (1992: 12) point to two other advantages of the connectionist approach:

First, we have a methodology in which the external world drives the computational model in a very direct, non-ad-hoc way. Second, we have a kind of system in which intelligent behaviour need not be grounded in any quasi-logical process of inferential reasoning about sentence-like structure representing states of the world. Intelligence and reasoning with quasi-linguistic structures thus come apart.

From these considerations it should be clear that I wish to argue that connectionist models are more useful for the understanding and modelling of complex systems than are rule-based models. I hope that this claim can be substantiated in the following chapters.

CONNECTIONISM AND POSTMODERNISM

One of the aims of this study is to show that some aspects of certain theories falling in the broad (and often mislabelled) category of 'postmodernism' have important implications for the study of complexity. These implications will be explored in more detail in the final chapter. They are only briefly introduced here.

Although Lyotard's *The Postmodern Condition* will form the basis of the discussion in Chapter 7, it is perhaps more accurate to say that the focus will be on the affinities between complexity theory and post-structural theory. The reason for this is that I wish to steer clear of those postmodern approaches that may be interpreted as relativistic. The central arguments will come from (mainly the early) work of Jacques Derrida (1973, 1976, 1978) – a position that can only be termed 'relativistic' by the ignorant.

Post-structural analyses are applied mostly to language, literature, culture and art, but the theoretical scope thereof is much wider. It is deeply concerned with an understanding and interpretation of our whole life-world, and therefore also has implications for our understanding of science. It is, however, rarely mentioned in the context of the philosophy of science, and the scientific community has paid little attention to these developments. This state of affairs is perhaps not surprising, if one considers the following two reasons:

- The great advances made in science, especially in the first half of the twentieth century, were modernist in nature. On a theoretical level, a strong alliance developed between science and those brands of philosophy that incorporated logic, such as logical positivism and its transformations (through Popper, Lakatos and Kuhn). In the context of both British analytical philosophy and American pragmatism, a philosophy of science developed with which scientists felt more or less comfortable. They thought that it reflected both their methods and aims. Since this analytical approach has virtually no implications for the actual practice of science, scientists could usually ignore philosophy, or at least not feel compelled to investigate alternative philosophical approaches.
- Post-structuralism (deconstruction) is often presented in anti-scientific terminology that stresses the proliferation of meaning, the breaking down of existing hierarchies, the shortcomings of logic, and the failures of analytical approaches. This subversive attitude is experienced as destructive, as throwing away all forms of rationality and thereby denying the very foundations of science. One cannot blame scientists for being sceptical about an approach that is (to my mind, incorrectly) presented in this way.

The first problem mentioned above results from a set of philosophical differences between analytical and continental philosophy. They should be addressed on the level of meaningful interaction between the two traditions. The second problem is the result of the *style* of thinking and writing prevalent in post-structural theory. In order to attract more serious attention from scientists, over-zealous post-structuralists (especially literary theorists) will have to transform their rhetoric into something cooler and clearer, something that can be argued with. Some post-structuralists may claim that such an approach is just not possible within 'true' post-structuralism, but that is a cop-out. My argument is that post-structuralism is not merely a subversive form of discourse analysis, but a style of thinking that is sensitive to the complexity of the phenomena under consideration. Since science can benefit from such an approach, the relevant ideas must be made accessible to scientists. Benefits would include the following:

- The narrow focus and reductionist tendency of the analytical approach can be impoverishing. The principle of falsification provides only a mechanism for getting rid of ideas. Post-structuralism, in contrast, is an inclusive approach that would actively encourage the generation of novel ideas, especially through trans-disciplinary interaction. Models from different disciplines can be transformed and incorporated, thereby increasing the options available in the pursuit of solutions to a specific problem.
- A post-structuralist approach would lead a philosophy of science to focus more on practical results – and the implications of these results – and less on the generation of an abstract meta-narrative that has to legitimate scientific knowledge.
- The general scientific 'method' can be replaced by something more sensitive to the contingencies of the issue at hand. In order to deal with observational and experimental data, often in vast quantities, science has traditionally placed great emphasis on following the correct method. Experiments are 'designed' in order to control the amount of variables and to restrict the possible interpretations of the results. Although this step can often not be avoided, it means that some of the possible results are eliminated *a priori*. Choosing a method is a pre-emptive move towards a specific set of solutions. Following a strict method has certainly provided marvellous results, but it often resulted in the *choice* of method receiving insufficient attention, and, moreover, has led to interpretation of experimental results in general terms, instead of within the framework of the appropriate method. Post-structuralism has a more 'playful' approach, but this attitude has nothing childish or frivolous about it. When dealing with complex phenomena, no single method will yield the whole truth. Approaching a complex system playfully allows for different avenues of advance, different viewpoints, and, perhaps, a better understanding of its characteristics.

Although I will emphasise the affinities between post-structuralism and a connectionist approach to complexity, none of the main arguments depends on first assuming a post-structural position. For that reason the subject matter of each chapter will be introduced and discussed without explicit reference to post-structuralism, even though those familiar with it should recognise the general strategy. For those unfamiliar with post-structural theory, an introduction to some of the relevant aspects of Derrida's thinking is provided in Chapter 3. Towards the end of each chapter the philosophical implications of the points made in that chapter will be discussed briefly. The final chapter will do so in detail.

MODELLING COMPLEXITY

In this chapter we have looked at some of the characteristics of complex systems in order to develop a sensitivity for the nature of complexity. This sensitivity is necessary when modelling complex systems, even if the model is a very limited one. The main points can be summarised in the following way:

- A closer look at the characteristics of complex systems clearly shows the limitations of the analytical method when dealing with complexity. There is nothing wrong with an analytical approach as such, but the 'analysis' of complex systems will always impose serious distortions by 'cutting out' part of the system.
- Algorithmic and information-theoretical approaches to complexity fail in their attempts to reveal the true nature of complexity, but provide us with one very valuable insight, namely that complexity is 'incompressible'. A complex system cannot be 'reduced' to a simple one unless it was not really complex to start with. A model of a complex system will have to 'conserve' the complexity of the system itself. Since the model will have to be as complex as the system it models, it cannot reveal the 'true nature' of the system in terms of a few logical principles.
- Complex systems have special relationships with their environment as far as the manner of processing information, and the developing and changing of internal structure, are concerned.
- Computer technology has opened up new possibilities for the modelling of complex systems. The conventional approach is to model the system in terms of a set of logical rules driving a formal symbol system. I have presented connectionist models as an alternative, and discussed different aspects of the two approaches.
- It was suggested that there are interesting links between connectionist models and post-structural theory. These links will be explored throughout this study.

In conclusion, I would like to motivate the choice of connectionist models of complexity again. A number of characteristics of complex systems were pointed out at the start of the chapter. Models of complex systems will have to capture them. In models based on formal symbol systems, these characteristics will have to be modelled explicitly. High levels of interconnectivity, recurrency, distributedness, etc., will have to be described algorithmically. In connectionist models these characteristics are already implicitly part of the structure of the model. The connectionist model *consists* of a large number of units, richly interconnected with feedback loops, but responding only to local information. In order to substantiate this claim, a slightly more technical introduction to neural networks will be given in the next chapter.

2   Introducing connectionism

I argue that the traditional rule-based and analytical approaches to complex systems are flawed, and that insights from postmodern and post-structural theory can help us to find novel ways of looking at complexity. The argument, however, does not remain on a purely theoretical level. There is also an attempt to show that these insights can influence our *models* of complex systems. The suggestion is that 'distributed' methods of modelling share some of the characteristics of complex systems, and that they therefore hold more promise than rule-based models, models which incorporate a strong theory of representation.

Neural networks, or connectionist models (as cognitive scientists like to refer to them), do not constitute the only 'distributed' modelling technique. Genetic algorithms and even cellular automata have similar characteristics. It is perhaps true that neural nets are particularly suitable because of their great flexibility, and this consideration has influenced the choice to use them as a paradigm example of distributed models.

Neural networks have important implications for a number of disciplines. In cognitive science, for example, connectionism caused a disturbance that some (Horgan and Tienson 1987: 97) would interpret as signs of a Kuhnian crisis. The wider *philosophical* implications of connectionism are underscored by the challenge it provides to some of the basic assumptions of artificial intelligence (AI) research, and in general to our understanding of the relationships between brain, mind and language. The importance of this modelling technique for the understanding of complex systems can be summarised in the following way:

- Neural networks conserve the complexity of the systems they model because they have complex structures themselves.
- Neural networks encode information about their environment in a distributed form. The notion of distributed representation undermines our understanding of conventional theories of representation.
- Neural networks have the capacity to self-organise their internal structure.

The latter two points will be dealt with in detail in Chapters 5 and 6. In this chapter I want to provide a general introduction to connectionism as well as situate the approach within a philosophical framework. A connectionist system that models certain linguistic capabilities is used as an example. The central part of the chapter examines an important critique of connectionism from an analytical perspective (Fodor and Pylyshyn 1988). The main concern in discussing the critique will be the role played by *rules* in linguistic and mental activities. The possibility of viewing connectionist models from a postmodern perspective will only be mentioned briefly, as it will be treated in more detail in the next chapter, where post-structuralism is introduced.

THEORETICAL BACKGROUND

Connectionism is a method of information-processing inspired by our understanding of the brain. Functionally the nervous system consists only of neurons. These cells are richly interconnected by means of synapses. The synapses convey the stimulation generated in a previous neuron to the dendrites of the next neuron in line. If this stimulation exceeds a certain threshold, the neuron is triggered and an impulse is sent down the axon of the neuron. This impulse in turn provides the synaptic input to a number of other neurons. The information passed from one neuron to the next is modified by the transfer characteristics of the synapses, as well as by the physical structure of the dendrites of the receiving neuron. Any single neuron receives inputs from, and provides inputs to, many others. Complex patterns of neural excitation seem to be the basic feature of brain activity.

A simple mathematical model of a neuron can be constructed. A neural unit uses the sum of its inputs to decide what output to generate. Each input is, however, first multiplied with a certain value or 'weight'. This weight determines the connection strength between two specific units, and models the characteristics of the synapses in the nervous system. The output response of any specific neuron (let us call it *A*) is therefore calculated in the following way: the outputs of all the neurons connected to *A* are – after having been multiplied in each case by the weight associated with the connection between that specific neuron and *A* – added together. This sum is multiplied with *A*'s transfer function to generate *A*'s output. This output becomes one of the inputs to the next neuron in the network, after it has in turn been adjusted by the value of the weight in that pathway. The value of the weight can be positive or negative. The transfer function is (in all but the most trivial cases) a non-linear function. Neurons form part of large networks with complex connection patterns, and since the weights determine the influence of one neuron on another, the characteristics of a network are mainly determined by the values of these weights.[1]

In a network, each neuron is continuously calculating its output in parallel with all the others, and patterns of activity, determined by the values of the weights, flow through the network. The topology of the

network, i.e. the way in which the neurons are interconnected, is also important. A network can be sparsely connected, richly connected or fully
connected. A fully interconnected network is one where every neuron is
connected to every other neuron. This configuration is known as a recurrent
net. Recurrent nets are extremely powerful, but difficult to work with.
Practical neural networks are structured more simply, usually in 'layers' of
neurons. A simple neural net is shown in Figure 2.1. This is an example of
what is usually referred to as a multi-layer perceptron. Information is
presented to the input layer and the result of the network's computations
can be found at the output layer. Between these two layers are one or more
'hidden' layers. They have no links with the outside world, but have to form
the associations between the input and the output.

In this network information flows only from the input side to the output
side, and the neurons are arranged in layers. Each neuron is connected to
every neuron in the next layer. Weights are not explicitly shown, but each
line has an associated weight. In this simple example, there are no connections between neurons in the same layer, and there are no feedback loops.
However, the activity of any specific neuron is influenced by many others,
and it in turn has an effect on many others. Information is therefore not
localised in any specific place in the network, but is distributed over a large
amount of units. The characteristics of the network are determined by the
two layers of weights.

We can now show how such a network, simple though it may be, is
capable of processing information. If the neurons in the input layer are activated in a certain way, a certain pattern will be generated by the output layer
as the input values are multiplied through the two layers of weights. The
input and the output can, of course, mean something. In the example we
will look at later, the input represents the present tense of English verbs, and
the output their past tense, as calculated by the network. If the network is

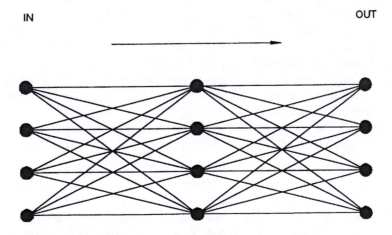

Figure 2.1 A simple feedforward neural network

presented with a verb, the pattern of weights will generate an output that represents (according to the network) its past tense. The crucial question at this point is the following: where do these weights, or at least, the value of each weight, come from? They could be predetermined by the designer of the network, but such predetermination is possible only in the case of the most simple problems and simple networks. However, it is not necessary for us to know the values of the weights beforehand. This is so because a network provided with enough examples of the problem it has to solve will generate the values of the weights by itself. A neural network is trained. It 'evolves' in the direction of a solution.

How is this done? By presenting the network with both the input pattern and the correct output, it can be made to adjust its weights in such a way as to match the two patterns closer. If sufficient examples are provided for long enough, and the network is complex enough to cope with the problem, a set of weights will be generated automatically that will produce the appropriate output for each input. After the network has been trained, it will not only recognise those examples it has been taught, but will take an educated guess in the case of unknown inputs as well. Because of the high degree of feedback, recurrent nets are not trained easily. For layered feedforward networks (simpler in structure, but still computationally powerful) there is a procedure, based on reducing the local error at each neuron, that guarantees convergence towards a solution (should there be one), provided that the network's structure has enough capacity to find it (i.e. that the network consists of enough neurons, particularly in the hidden layer). This is known as the back-propagation procedure.

Let me summarise the basic theory of connectionist models by pointing to a few crucial features. A neural network consists of large numbers of simple neurons that are richly interconnected. The weights associated with the connections between neurons determine the characteristics of the network. During a training period, the network adjusts the values of the interconnecting weights. The value of any specific weight has no significance; it is the patterns of weight values in the whole system that bear information. Since these patterns are complex, and are generated by the network itself (by means of a general learning strategy applicable to the whole network), there is no abstract procedure available to describe the process used by the network to solve the problem. There are only complex patterns of relationships.

A few more examples of how neural networks perform some general, but fairly complex tasks, will illustrate various aspects of their capacities.

- Even simple networks, as the one in Figure 2.1, can perform *classification* tasks. Consider a number of different classes, each with its own members. The output neurons of a network can each be taken to stand for a specific class. During the training phase, different examples of each class are presented as input to the network. With every particular input the output neuron associated with the appropriate class is switched on. In this way the network learns to associate all the members of a class with a specific output. If the training examples are representative of the various classes, the network will be able to do a reliable classification, even of examples that did not form part of the training set.

Classification tasks like these are often called 'pattern recognition'. An example of the latter would be a network that can recognise different types of vehicles by the noise they make. By training the network with, for example, the noise-spectrum produced by a group of motorbikes, motorcars and trucks, the network will learn to distinguish between them. If the training examples were representative of each class, the network will afterwards be able to classify a specific type of motorcar as motorcar, even if it has not encountered that specific type before. The network does not develop a specific *algorithm* for performing the recognition task; it merely multiplies the input information through the network. The correct configuration of weights, developed during the training phase, produces the required output. The same network can be retrained to perform a completely different task.

- A network can perform a *mapping*. A certain input configuration can be transformed into a certain output configuration. This is a generalisation of the classification capabilities. In this case the output of the network does not consist of only one active neuron, indicating a specific class, but a pattern of activity spread over the whole output layer. The nature of the mapping is constrained only by the complexity of the network. If the network is complex enough, an arbitrary mapping can be performed (Hornick *et al.* 1989). An example of such a mapping is the network that transforms present tense verbs into their past tense form, discussed in more detail below.

- A network can perform *curve-fitting*. Consider a function of the following form: $y = f(x_1, x_2, x_3 \ldots x_n)$. If the input neurons are provided with the values of x_1 to x_n, an output neuron can provide an approximation of y, provided that the network is complex enough to approximate the function f. The network is taught with correct values of y for given values of x. If the training examples are representative, the network will accurately 'fit' a set of input values to a curve that approximates f. Note that it is not necessary to know what f is. Given a set of xs and the corresponding values for y, the network will generate a set of weights that perform the curve-fitting automatically. It should, however, come as no surprise that these networks are better at interpolation than at extrapolation. These networks are often used to perform control functions and also as predictors, e.g. in stock-market analysis.

- Neural networks can perform automatic *clustering*. Given a two-dimensional array of neurons, with each one receiving the same set of input values, the network will cluster input vectors $(x_1, x_2 \ldots x_n)$ that are close together by activating neurons that are close together. This is achieved through a process of internal competition that causes the network to self-organise its internal structure. This capability of neural networks is analysed in detail in Chapter 6.

The way in which neural networks solve problems has some philosophical importance. In order to make this more apparent, I will place connectionism in a more general theoretical framework. Two paradigms can be identified, each one associated with the name of a famous linguist – the one Noam Chomsky, the other Ferdinand de Saussure. Such a dichotomy is always somewhat artificial and simplistic, but it is useful in linking styles of information-processing with certain intellectual traditions. The link between connectionism and contemporary continental theory is an especially fruitful one since it allows us to engage with postmodern theories from a different perspective. The two paradigms are summarised in Table 2.1.

The way the Chomskian paradigm sticks together is well known. The formal grammars of production rules Chomsky employs to describe language are identical to the mathematical models developed by Alan Turing. These models, known as Turing machines,[2] also provide the mathematical foundation for the description of digital computers. Hilary Putnam proposed that the Turing machine is an adequate model of the brain (a theory that has become known as functionalism, and which Putnam [1988] no longer supports), and Jerry Fodor (1975) extended Chomsky's rationalist programme by linking the rule-based system of language with the functional working of the mind, irrespective of the hardware in which it is implemented. This is the paradigm that formed the basis for cognitive science and artificial intelligence (AI) research. It is only to be expected that within such a paradigm intelligent behaviour should be described as rule-following, and hence we have the rule-based AI simulations known as expert systems.

The paradigm identified with the name of Saussure is not often associated with computational theory. One reason may be the fact that cognitive science in general, and connectionism in particular, is practised in a context where Saussurian principles are unfamiliar. Part of the aim of this book is

Table 2.1 Two paradigms of information-processing

Chomsky	*Saussure*
Models of language and the mind work with systems of production rules and are explained in formal and representational terms (Fodor)	Models of language and the brain work with systems of relationships and are not understood in representational terms (Freud, Lacan, Derrida)
Mathematical model supplied by Turing machine	Mathematical model supplied by connectionist networks
Machine-produced: digital computer	Machine-produced: neural network
'Intelligent' application: expert systems	'Intelligent' application: pattern recognition

to establish the sensibility of such a paradigm. There are relationships between Saussure's description of language (where each element of a language only has meaning in terms of the degrees to which it differs from all the other elements of a language), and the way the brain works, especially when the way Saussurian theory was elaborated and criticised by post-structural thinkers like Jacques Derrida (discussed in more detail in Chapter 3) is taken into account. One could possibly use neural network theory to provide a mathematical description of Saussurian linguistics, equivalent to the way in which formal grammars provide the mathematical description of Chomskian linguistics. Here I am primarily concerned with connectionism as a general model for complex systems and I will also attempt to show that there are important differences between connectionist and conventional models. These differences hinge to a large extent on the role and status of the *rule*, especially as far as language is concerned.

THE RULES OF LANGUAGE

As part of their seminal connectionist research programme, David Rumelhart and James McClelland developed a neural network that generates the past tense of the present tense English verbs it is presented with (Rumelhart and McClelland 1986, Vol. 2: 216–271). They did not develop a large-scale linguistic system, but chose an area of language that was confined enough to be manageable, yet rich enough to allow them to argue their position. The generation of past tense forms of verbs is usually described by a fair number of rules, and a fair number of irregularities are also present.

The network they employed was a simple feedforward network similar to the one described above. The input and output layers each consisted of 460 neurons (239). During the learning phase the network was presented with phonological representations of the present tense of English verbs at the input layer, and the representation of the past tense at the output layer. At each presentation the weights of the network were adjusted using a process known as the 'perceptron convergence procedure' (225), also known as back-propagation. The output generated by the network for each input was constantly monitored throughout the learning phase. It was found that the network captured most of the features of both regular and irregular verbs in the same collection of weights, and that the network could respond appropriately to verbs it had not encountered before. Furthermore, during the training phase the network performed in ways similar to the way in which children acquire the past tense (219, 240). A child at first knows only the small number of past tense verbs that are often used. Most of these are irregular, but are used correctly. In a second phase certain patterns are noticed, and a process of over-regularisation takes place. More verbs are used, but irregular verbs, previously used correctly, are now regularised. In a third phase the differences are noticed, and regular and irregular forms are allowed to co-exist. These three phases were mimicked by Rumelhart and McClelland's network. This kind of performance by a network that only employs patterns of association led them to the following conclusion:

> We have, we believe, provided a distinct alternative to the view that children learn the rules of English past-tense formation in any explicit sense. We have shown that a reasonable account of the acquisition of past tense can be provided without recourse to the notion of a 'rule' as anything more than a *description* of the language.
>
> (267)

That is, even though rules may be useful to describe linguistic phenomena, explicit rules need not be employed when language is acquired or when it is used. These unorthodox claims were sure to generate a response from the Chomskian camp. In what follows we take a look at how Jerry Fodor and Zenon Pylyshyn dismissed connectionism as a model for cognition and language.

The context in which Fodor and Pylyshyn (1988) enter the discussion is one in which connectionist systems are contrasted with symbol systems. In a symbol system information is represented by discrete symbols that are structured and manipulated by means of rules. The nature of a symbol system is determined by that which the symbols *represent*, and not by the way in which the system is implemented. If a biological system and a digital computer manipulate the same symbols in the same way, they are functionally equivalent.

Fodor and Pylyshyn identify two major traditions in 'modern theorizing about the mind'. They call the one 'Representationalist' and the other 'Eliminativist'.

> Representationalists hold that postulating representational (or 'intentional' or 'semantic') states is essential to a theory of cognition; according to Representationalists, there are states of the mind which function to encode states of the world. Eliminativists, by contrast, think that psychological theories can dispense with such semantic notions as representation. According to Eliminativists the appropriate vocabulary for psychological theorizing is neurological or, perhaps behavioural, or perhaps syntactic; in any event, not a vocabulary that characterizes mental states in terms of what they represent.
>
> (Fodor and Pylyshyn 1988: 7)

Strangely enough, they then claim that 'connectionist modelling is consistently Representationalist' (8), and therefore on the same side of the divide as 'classical' cognitive theory, the position they defend. The only difference between them, on this issue, is that classicists assign semantic content to 'expressions', and that connectionists assign it to nodes in a network. They therefore claim that 'representation' is not part of the dispute. What then are the issues? This is how they summarise it:

Classical and Connectionist theories disagree about the nature of mental representation; for the former, but not for the latter, mental representations characteristically exhibit a combinatorial constituent structure and a combinatorial semantics. Classical and Connectionist theories also disagree about the nature of mental processes; for the former, but not for the latter, mental processes are characteristically sensitive to the combinatorial structure of the representations on which they operate.

(32)

What do these two differences amount to? A representational system works with symbols. For symbols to be meaningful, they firstly have to be *structured*, and, secondly, it must be possible to *manipulate* them. Unrelated collections of symbols are meaningless. Connectionist systems are representational, but because they merely 'associate' representations, and have no rules to manipulate them with, they cannot model the mind.

What's deeply wrong with Connectionist architecture is this: Because it acknowledges neither syntactic nor semantic structure in mental representations, it perforce treats them not as a generated set but as a list. But lists, qua lists, have no structure; any collection of items is a possible list. And, correspondingly, on Connectionist principles, any collection of (causally connected) representational states is a possible mind. So, as far as Connectionist architecture is concerned, there is nothing to prevent minds that are arbitrarily unsystematic. But that result is *preposterous*. Cognitive capacities come in structurally related clusters; their systematicity is pervasive.

(49)

Their objections certainly hold water if one is committed to a system built up out of atomic representations. They are, however, gravely mistaken in thinking that connectionist systems fit that description. By insisting that information is represented in the *nodes* of a network (12), they miss the real significance of the distributed representations in neural networks, a point also made by Smolensky (1987: 137), Derthick (1990: 255, 257) and Bechtel (1987: 22). The example with which Fodor and Pylyshyn choose to demonstrate a connectionist network is not a neural network at all. It is a semantic network, a well-known technique from traditional AI that merely depicts a few relationships between a number of atomic representations.[3] They acknowledge the existence of distributed representations, but for them it is merely local representations 'sliced thinner'. The point, however, is the following: in a full-blown neural network no node has any specific significance. As explained earlier, the significance lies in the values of the *weights*; not, and this is crucial, in the value of any specific weight or even group of weights, but in the way they are related and activated each time. Information is not stored in – or rather, represented by – a symbol and recalled when necessary (as in traditional cognitive models), but is reconstructed each time that that part of the network is activated (Bechtel 1987: 22).

Smolensky (1987) would argue that distributed representation is representation of some form, but so different to the classical models that they cannot be placed under the same heading. The differences between the two systems are far more radical than Fodor and Pylyshyn would admit, and the argument has to be taken up on a different level. For now, one can say that in terms of the limited networks currently used to demonstrate connectionist principles or to solve specific problems, Smolensky is correct. These networks address well-specified problems, in other words, problems that are well framed. As models they do represent their problem areas, even if it is in some unconventional way. When we move to large systems where the frame is less apparent, I am convinced that the concept of mental representation has to be dropped altogether. In a certain sense the meaning of the word 'representation' breaks down if used in the context of a 'distributed representation'. Objects in the world are not 'represented' in the brain, just as a word in a natural language does not 'represent' a specific meaning. This claim will be argued for in Chapter 5.

Despite the problem of representation, one could of course pose the question as to whether the connectionist approach and rule-based one exclude each other; whether the one cannot be reduced to the other. Fodor and Pylyshyn (1988: 64) acknowledge the biological plausibility of connectionist architectures, and the fact that neural nets can be used to implement a Turing machine. They suggest this as a possible option, and then urge connectionists to direct their research at achieving good implementations of 'classical' architectures.[4] This strategy, however, denies the important differences between local representations and fully distributed systems. Smolensky (1987: 137–143) suggests five possible ways of dealing with the 'soft' connectionist option, on the one hand, and the 'hard' symbol system, on the other:

- Deny one and continue only with the other. The denial of the 'soft' is also known as 'rationalism'. Denial of the 'hard' leads (according to Smolensky) to the 'intuitive' approaches of for example Dreyfus and Dreyfus (1986).
- Allow the two systems to 'cohabitate' as two separate 'processors' next to each other. In a way this is an extreme formulation of the split brain theory.
- Soften the 'hard' approach by means of fuzzy logic. This merely blurs the edges, and softness becomes *degrees* of hardness.
- Make the system which is 'hard' at bottom complex enough that softness will emerge. This is a sophisticated approach, but the 'brittleness' of expert systems with many rules remains discouraging.
- Make a system which is 'soft' at bottom complex enough that hardness will *sometimes* appear when viewed at a higher level.

I find the last suggestion most intriguing. It postulates a system that does not function on the basis of rules, but where certain systematic properties can be *described* by means of rules if they prove to be useful. I cannot see why this suggestion should not satisfy those who like to look for structures and patterns.[5] They can make interesting and useful classifications without claiming to have discovered essential components that can be elevated to Final Truths. I suspect, however, that this will be a problematic position for the True Scientist, for whom, like Fodor and Pylyshyn (1988: 64), 'truth is more important than respectability'.[6]

CONNECTIONISM AND POSTMODERN SCIENCE

The relationships between science, postmodern theory and connectionist models of complex systems will be examined in the final chapter. However, there are a few remarks to be made here, in the context of cognitive science.

In many areas of science, both theoretical and applied, there is a growing discontent with analytical and deterministic methods and descriptions. One of the first responses to this unease was a rapid growth in statistical approaches, not only in the interpretation of experiments, but in the explanation of the results as well. However, as in the case of fuzzy logic, statistical methods do not imply a break with deterministic methods. It remains a tool in the process of establishing the *true* mechanisms of the phenomena being investigated. The heavy price paid in the process – that of averaging out the complex internal detail – is usually glossed over.

To think in terms of relationships, rather than in terms of deterministic rules, is not a novelty for science, but it has always been seen as part of qualitative descriptions and not as part of the quantitative descriptions and calculations deemed necessary ever since Kepler's insistence that 'to measure is to know'. Many phenomena, especially in the life-sciences, but also in physics and mathematics, simply cannot be understood properly in terms of deterministic, rule-based or statistical processes. Quantum-mechanical descriptions of sub-atomic processes are essentially relational, and even on a more macroscopic level, relations determine the nature of matter. The carbon atoms in my body can all be interchanged with carbon atoms from the wood of my desktop, and there will be no noticeable difference (Penrose 1989: 32). The significance of each atom is therefore not determined by its basic nature, but is a result of a large number of relationships between itself and other atoms.

In the light of these examples, it is certainly strange that when it comes to descriptions of the functioning of the brain, an obviously relational structure, there is still such a strong adherence to atomic representation and deterministic algorithms. One of the reasons for this must surely be that cognitive science inherited its methodological framework from a deterministic, analytical tradition. Post-structural theory, I claim, assists us in revising this position.

The interaction between post-structuralism and cognitive science could have mutual benefits. On a methodological level, a post-structural approach could affirm the non-algorithmic nature of cognition. It could help to suppress the desire to find complete and deterministic models by arguing that models based on a system of relationships are less restrictive, and just as useful. It can also help to legitimise activities that aspire not to fill in the 'big picture', but only to be of local use. One can also argue for a number of interesting similarities between connectionism and Derrida's model of language (as will be done in the next chapter). If post-structural arguments can help us to implement better models of complex systems, it will help to dispel the delivered opinion that post-structural concepts are confined to the realm of theory and have no practical value.

3   Post-structuralism, connectionism and complexity

The primary aim of this chapter is to introduce post-structuralism in order to point out its relevance for the study of complex systems. This will be done by means of a discussion of the theory of language proposed by Saussure (1974), as criticised and developed by Derrida (1976). Those familiar with this body of thought may like to proceed to the latter sections of the chapter where the links with complexity theory and connectionist networks are discussed.

Saussure's 'structural' model of language remains a landmark in the study of complex systems. His primary insight – that meaning is generated through a system of differences – remains an excellent way of conceptualising the relationships in a complex system. His model is somewhat 'rigid', but Derrida's transformation of the system by means of a sophisticated description of how the relationships interact in time (using the notion of *différance*) provides us with an excellent way of conceptualising the dynamics of complex systems from a philosophical perspective. Moreover, I wish to argue that recurrent connectionist networks can be used to model this general conceptualisation.

The central argument of the book can therefore be summarised in the following way:

- Complexity is best characterised as arising through large-scale, non-linear interaction.
- Since it is based on a system of relationships, the post-structural inquiry into the nature of language helps us to theorise about the dynamics of the interaction in complex systems. In other words, the dynamics that generates meaning in language can be used to describe the dynamics of complex systems in general.
- Connectionist networks share the characteristics of complex systems, including those aspects described by a post-structural theory of language. It should therefore be possible to use them (or other distributed modelling techniques with similar capabilities) as general models for complex systems. These models can be physically implemented or simulated computationally.

In order to give substance to this argument, I will first introduce the post-structural conceptualisation of language.

SAUSSURE'S MODEL OF LANGUAGE

Most models of language, but specifically the Chomskian one, focus on the *structure* of language. In his *Course in General Linguistics*, Saussure's main concern was the *meaning* of language. How do words acquire meaning? He did argue that language consists of a number of discrete units, which he called *signs*, but rather than ascribing characteristics to the signs themselves, he concentrated on the relationships between them.[1]

For Saussure the sign consists of two components: the signifier and the signified. The signifier is the linguistic unit and the signified is the concept it represents. The signifier and the signified, however, are not separable entities. 'The linguistic sign is a two-sided psychological entity that . . . unites not a thing and a name, but a concept and a sound-image' (Saussure 1974: 66). For example, the word 'tree' would be a signifier in the English language and the concept of a tree would be the signified. Together they form the sign for tree. Language is a system of such signs.

The sign also has, according to Saussure (1974: 67), two 'primordial' characteristics. The first is the most important: there is no *natural* link between a signifier and a signified. The relationship between the concept of a tree and the word 'tree' is not given outside language, it is purely arbitrary. This does not mean that the individual speaker can *choose* the word for a concept, but rather that the relationship is 'unmotivated' (69), i.e. it exists merely as a convention in language. The second characteristic Saussure mentions is that the sign unfolds linearly in time. This characteristic does not seem to be important for his theory as a whole, but it does underline his insistence on the spoken form of language as primary – an issue we will return to later.

How is it possible for signs to have meaning if their nature is conventional, but, at the same time, not by choice or by the definition of a collection of individual speakers? By being part of a system. 'Where there are signs there is system' (Culler 1976: 91). The system of language is constituted not by individual speech acts, but by a system of relationships that transcends the individual user. This system is what Saussure calls '*langue*', as opposed to language in use, '*parole*' (Saussure 1974: 13, 14). Because the signifier–signified relationship is arbitrary, the sign does not have a natural identity, but has to derive its significance from the relationships within the system.

To explain the way in which these relationships work, Saussure uses the example of a train, say the '8.25 Geneva-to-Paris' (108). Although the train itself, its personnel and its passengers are different every day, the '8.25 Geneva-to-Paris' maintains its identity by its relationships to the '8.40 Geneva-to-Dijon', the '12.00 Geneva-to-Paris', or the '0.38 Bombay-to-

Madras', for that matter, irrespective of whether it leaves at 8.25 exactly, or reaches Paris in the same state as when it left. The train does not have any identity by itself; its identity is determined relationally. Similarly, a linguistic sign derives its meaning from its relationships to other signs. The signifier 'brown' does not have a meaning because it can be identified with a concept that unambiguously contains the essence of 'brownness', but because it can be differentiated from the signifiers 'black', 'blue', 'grey', 'hard', 'train', etc. The sign is determined by the way in which it *differs* from all the other signs in the system – 'in language there are only differences without positive terms' (120). The sign is a node in a network of relationships. The relationships are not determined by the sign; rather, the sign is the *result* of interacting relationships.

Saussure does acknowledge that the relationships between signifiers change and therefore he distinguishes between the diachronic and synchronic study of language. A synchronic study would look at the system as it is at a given point in time, while a diachronic study will try to show how a certain state of the system was arrived at historically. Change, however, is highly controlled. Saussure emphasises this in two (seemingly contradictory) ways. On the one hand, he insists on the *immutability* of the sign:

> The signifier, though to all appearances freely chosen with respect to the idea that it represents, is fixed, not free, with respect to the linguistic community that uses it. The masses have no voice in the matter and the signifier chosen by language could be replaced by no other. This fact, which seems to embody a contradiction, might be called colloquially 'the stacked deck'. No individual, even if he willed it, could modify in any way at all the choice that has been made; and what is more, the community itself cannot control so much as a single word; it is bound to the existing language.
>
> (71)

The system of language transcends the choices of any individual user, and therefore has stability. Because the users of language have to operate within the system of language they inherited, and because their understanding of language is constituted by that system, they cannot break out of it. The system perpetuates itself in a way that guarantees its integrity. That is what Saussure means when referring to language as 'the stacked deck'. On the other hand, he also insists on the *mutability* of the sign:

> Time, which insures the continuity of language, wields another influence apparently contradictory to the first: the more or less rapid change of linguistic signs. In a certain sense, therefore, we can speak of both the immutability and the mutability of the sign. In the last analysis, the two facts are interdependent: the sign is exposed to alteration because it perpetuates itself. What predominates in all change is the persistence of the old substance; disregard for the past is only

relative. That is why the principle of change is based on the principle of continuity.

(74)

This apparent contradiction is a result of the arbitrary nature of the sign. If the sign had a natural or essential meaning, it would always remain exactly the same. If it was up to an individual speaker to reallocate the meaning, the meaning would change instantaneously when the signifier becomes associated with another signified. Neither of these two possibilities reflects the way language works. Because the relationship is arbitrary, and only has significance in terms of the *system*, there is no 'essence', nor is there instantaneous change of isolated signs. 'Regardless of what the forces of change are, whether in isolation or in combination, they always result in a shift in the relationship between the signified and the signifier' (75). Change can only be traced in terms of the difference that is produced between a previous and a new set of relationships, and this is the result of an evolutionary process. Saussure has the following to say about the evolution of language:

> Nothing could be more complex. As it is a product of both the social force and time, no one can change anything in it, and on the other hand, the arbitrariness of its signs theoretically entails the freedom of establishing just any relationship between phonetic substance and ideas. The result is that each of the two elements united in the sign maintains its own life to a degree unknown elsewhere, and that language changes, or rather evolves, under the influence of all the forces which can affect either sounds or meanings. The evolution is inevitable; there is no example of a single language that resists it. After a certain period of time, some obvious shifts can always be recorded.
>
> (76)

Saussure's argument is that language, even an artificial language like Esperanto, can only be controlled as long as it is not in circulation. As soon as it is used by a community, it will adapt and change. Saussure also insists that the system as a whole is never modified directly, but only *elements* of the system (84). The changed elements, however, interact with the rest of the system, and in such a way the whole system is eventually changed. The result is not a new, completely different system, but rather a transformation of the old system (85). There is also no external telos that provides a direction for change; change is the result of contingencies arising in the context where language is used. This context, Saussure (77, 78) stresses quite explicitly, is the social context provided by the community of speakers who use the language. In terms of a general theory of complex systems, one would say that these dynamics of the system of language are a result of the way in which the system self-organises in order to meet the needs of the community (see Chapter 6).

Despite his description of the linguistic domain as a system of differences in which the elements are constituted only by their relationships, Saussure insists on a number of general distinctions within that domain. Apart from the distinction between signifier and signified, there are distinctions between the synchronic and the diachronic, the morphological and the phonological, and the syntagmatic and the paradigmatic. Syntagmatic relations are those which concern the specific *sequence* in which a number of linguistic signs are used to form a sentence. Paradigmatic relations are those which apply between a sign and all the other signs that could replace it. It is as if the system of relations does not satisfy his need to describe language. He has to add a set of general distinctions to provide a stronger structure, even though he realises that none of these distinctions functions on its own. There is always a dialectical relationship between the opposites (Culler 1976: 50).

A further unexpected element of Saussure's description of language is his insistence on the primacy of spoken language over written language. For Saussure (1974: 24–25), writing is but an image of the signs which find their true manifestation in the spoken form. It is an image that obscures the true nature of the sign to such an extent that he refers to it as 'the tyranny of writing' (31). If one adds to this insistence on the importance of spoken language his original definition of the sign as a 'psychological entity' (66), language acquires a personal, subjective nature that is opposed to his description of it as a transpersonal system. It is as if Saussure on the one hand denies that a sign has an essential nature, but on the other hand insists that the individual speaker somehow gets it right. This tension will be examined further in the next section where we look at the way in which Derrida argues for the primacy of writing. Saussure's insistence on the priority of spoken language results in giving priority to the mental state of the speaker, to the concept she/he has in mind, and therefore to the signified. The signifier becomes the token of the signified, its representation. However, with an insistence on the primacy of writing, this process is reversed: now the signified has no special status, it becomes another signifier whose meaning is not present when it is used, but has to be traced through the whole system of interacting signifiers.

LANGUAGE AS A SYSTEM OF SIGNIFIERS ONLY

Saussure introduced a system of language in which linguistic components are not assigned identity by means of rules, but derive their meaning from their relationships with all the other components. At first glance this appears to entail a fairly radical shift. However, if one considers Saussure's insistence on both the stability of the system and the evolution of the system in a *linear* temporal dimension, it becomes clear that the mechanisms of the system can be given a fairly conventional description. Harland (1987: 136) describes it as a 'simultaneous system' in the following way:

... all words together stand still and stable in a total simultaneous system. Simultaneous, in that the system only balances if words push against each other at exactly the same time; total, in that the system only balances if there are no internal gaps to give words room for falling, and no surrounding void to give words room for dispersing. For a state of perfect equilibrium, words need to be packed tightly up together within a closed space.

Ultimately, Saussure understands language as a system in which every word has its place, and, consequently, its meaning. The system does evolve, but it remains in a state near equilibrium. However, complex systems, like language, do not operate near equilibrium, and the relationships between the components of the system are non-linear and dynamic. Words, or signs, do not have fixed positions. The relationships between signs are not stable enough for each sign to be determined exactly. In a way, interaction is only possible if there is some 'space' between signs. There are always more possibilities than can be actualised (Luhmann 1985: 25). The meaning of a sign is the result of the 'play' in the space between signs. Signs in a complex system always have an excess of meaning, with only some of the potential meaning realised in specific situations.

How do we talk about systems with characteristics like these? How do we describe the dynamics of interaction if the components are not fixed in a 'simultaneous system'? In an attempt to answer these questions, a look at Derrida's deconstruction of Saussure might be helpful.

Derrida's critique of Saussure's description of the sign is related to his critique of a tendency in the whole tradition of Western philosophy, which he calls the 'metaphysics of presence'. In the case of Saussure, the metaphysics of presence is affirmed by his insistence that the sign has two components, the signifier and the signified, of which one, the signified, is mental or psychological (Saussure 1974: 66). This would imply that the meaning of a sign is *present* to the speaker when he uses it, in defiance of the fact that meaning is constituted by a system of differences. That is also why Saussure insists on the primacy of speaking. As soon as language is written down, a distance between the subject and his words is created, causing meaning to become unanchored.

Derrida, however, argues that Saussure has no reason to be anxious about this state of affairs. He insists that the distance between the subject and his words exists in any case; that the meaning of the sign is always unanchored, even when we speak. Thus, the signified (or 'mental' component) never has any immediate self-present meaning. It is itself only a sign that derives its meaning from other signs. Such a viewpoint entails that the sign is, in a sense, stripped of its 'signified' component. Since the signified is also constituted through a system of relationships, it functions just like a signifier. The signified is nothing but another signifier that has to take its position in the endless interaction between signifiers. Meaning is never simply present and therefore we cannot escape the process of interpretation, even when the speaker is in front of us. That is why Derrida chooses writing – the 'signifier of the signifier' (Derrida 1976: 7), that which always already has distance – as a model of the linguistic system:

> Now from the moment that one considers the totality of determined signs, spoken, and a fortiori, written, as unmotivated institutions, one must exclude any relationship of natural subordination, any natural hierarchy among signifiers or orders of signifiers. If 'writing' signifies inscription and especially the durable institution of a sign (and that is the only irreducible kernel of the concept of writing), writing in general covers the entire field of linguistic signs.
>
> (Derrida 1976: 44)

The deconstruction of the sign, i.e. the removal of its mental component, is closely linked to the deconstruction of the subject and of consciousness. In both cases the deconstruction resists the notion of presence. If there is no signified whose content is immediately present to consciousness, but only signifiers whose meaning is unstable and excessive, then the content of consciousness becomes excessive; it cannot be made complete. The subject is no longer in control of meaning that can be made present, but is itself *constituted* by the play of signifiers.

Put in the language of systems theory, Saussure still understands language as a closed system, whereas Derrida wants to argue for language as an open system. In denying the metaphysics of presence, the distinction between 'inside' and 'outside' is also problematised. There is no place outside of language from where meaning can be generated. Where there is meaning, there is already language. We cannot separate language from the world it describes. 'The outside bears with the inside a relationship that is, as usual, anything but simple exteriority. The meaning of the outside was always present within the inside, imprisoned outside the outside, and vice versa' (Derrida 1976: 35). Only when the distinction between inside and outside is ruptured, can the system become an open one.

If the system of language is as open as Derrida suggests, if the relationships are always playfully changing in an unpredictable way, how is it possible to say anything about these relationships? In some sense we cannot say anything permanent and specific about them that would apply to language in general. The play of signifiers does, however, create 'pockets of stability' (Stofberg 1988: 224), otherwise communication could not get started. Within these pockets a more rigorous analysis of relationships is possible, as long as it is understood that the stability is not permanent or complete, that meaning remains a result of the *process* of interaction between signifiers. This interaction is explained by Derrida in terms of, amongst others, two concepts: 'trace' and '*différance*'. He stresses that they are actually neither concepts nor words (Derrida 1982: 7), that they cannot be given a full meaning. Perhaps Derrida is complicating matters unnecessarily, but his intention seems to be to prevent these two terms from acquiring fixed meanings. It is by their very instability that they allow us to say something more general about language. I will attempt to describe these terms in a meaningful way.

Saussure defines the meaning of a sign in terms of the relationships it has with all the other signs in the system. For example, the meaning of the sign 'brown' is determined not only by the way in which it differs from the signs 'blue', 'green' and 'red', but also by the way it differs from signs like 'dog', 'spring' and 'unwieldy'. The sign has no component that belongs to itself only; it is merely a collection of the traces of every other sign running through it. This is emphasised by Derrida. The sign is an entity without any positive content. Because it is constituted by nothing more than relationships, it consists only of traces. The implication is clearly that the traces constituting a specific sign do not emanate from *other* signs that are self-sufficient and therefore have some positive content to bestow. On the contrary, all signs are constituted by the system of differences.

> The play of differences involves syntheses and referrals that prevent there from being at any moment or in any way a simple element that is present in and of itself and refers only to itself. Whether in written or in spoken discourse, no element can function as a sign without relating to another element which itself is not simply present. This linkage means that each 'element' – phoneme or grapheme – is constituted with reference to the trace in it of the other elements of the sequence or system. This linkage, this weaving, is the text, which is produced only through the transformation of another text. Nothing, either in the elements or in the system, is anywhere simply present or absent. There are only, everywhere, differences and traces of traces.
>
> (Derrida 1981: 26)

There are no fixed reference-points from where traces emanate, neither spatially nor temporally. It is not possible to trace the origin of the trace synchronically or diachronically. One can attempt to track down the various routes of the trace, but one will never arrive at a starting-place or an origin which is not already divided by difference.[2]

It is one thing to describe the sign as consisting only of traces, but it should also be possible to say something about the 'mechanism' of *interaction* of the trace. Here our understanding of the dynamics of complex systems can be enhanced by Derrida's notion of '*différance*'. This a complex notion with several layers of meaning. It refers in the first place to the description of language as a system of *differences*. Traces are traces of difference. In the play of differences meaning is generated. However, as this play is always in progress, meaning is never produced finally, but continuously *deferred*. As soon as a certain meaning is generated for a sign, it reverberates through the system. Through the various loops and pathways, this disturbance in the traces is reflected back on the sign in question, shifting its 'original' meaning, even if only imperceptibly. Because no trace is in a privileged position, the word 'defer' can be read not only in the temporal sense, but also in the sense of 'submitting to'. Each trace is not only delayed, but also subjugated by every other trace.

The mechanism of interaction between traces entails still more than differing/deferring. The mechanism is not a passive characteristic of the system, nor the result of a positive act. The process of *différance* remains suspended somewhere between active and passive. The sign is produced by the system, but is at the same time also involved in the production of the system. The characteristics of the system emerge as a result of the *différance* of traces, not as a result of essential characteristics of specific components of the system.[3]

An element of *différance* that is not apparent from its polysemia is that of 'spacing'. In order for signs to interact by means of traces and *différance*, they cannot, as we have seen above, be stacked tightly against each other. Space is required as a site of action. The suspension between active and passive is apparent here as well: *différance* can only take place if there is a certain space, a space maintained through the dynamics of *différance*. *Différance* thus has both spatial and temporal characteristics (see Derrida 1982: 13).

Both concepts, trace and *différance*, are employed to say something about the inner workings of language, or rather – since language becomes the model of any system of interacting signs – of all complex systems. In what follows I will argue for specific links between the post-structural theory and network models of complexity.

NETWORKS AND SYSTEMS

At about the same time that Saussure developed his theory of language (around the turn of the century), Freud proposed a model for the functioning of the brain. This early work, known as the *Project for a Scientific Psychology* – published posthumously (Freud 1950) – is not as well known as his mature works, but it remains indispensable for a full understanding of Freud. What is more, as far as the functioning of the brain is concerned, it is largely compatible with contemporary neurological theory (see Pribram and Gill 1976).

Freud's model consists of neurons that interact through pathways which channel the energy in the brain. This energy comes both from outside the body (perception), and from internal sources. Pathways resist the flow of energy, unless it is used often (here we have one of the earliest formulations of the 'use-principle', or Hebb's rule). The characteristics of the brain are determined by the various patterns of energy flowing through it. Two important aspects of this model deserve attention. In the first place the role of *memory* should be underscored. 'Memory' refers here to the physical condition of the brain: which pathways are breached ('facilitated') and which are not. Memory is not a cognitive function performed by a conscious subject, but an unconscious characteristic of the brain (which is an organ, part of the body). Memory is the substrate that sets up the conditions for all the functions of the brain.

The second important characteristic of Freud's model concerns the role of the neurons. No neuron is significant by itself. Memory does not reside *in* any neuron, but in the relationship between neurons. This relationship, Freud (1950: 300) declares, is one of *differences*. What we have, therefore, is a model structurally equivalent to Saussure's model of language: a system of differences.[4] Taking Derrida's reading of both Freud and Saussure as a cue, we can develop a description of the dynamics of networks of interacting neurons, using the theoretical equipment developed in the post-structural approach to language.

Derrida uses the concept of 'trace' to point to the influence that each component in the system of language has on every other component. The notion of trace is intimately linked with the notion of memory – memory in the material, non-subjective sense described above. In a neural network the function of memory is performed by the weights of the relationships between neurons. Because of the 'distributed' nature of these relationships, a specific weight has no ideational content, but only gains significance in large patterns of interaction. It therefore seems fruitful to suggest that the two terms – 'weight' and 'trace' – can in this context be used to describe each other. To think of weights in a neural network as *traces* (in Derrida's sense) helps to understand how meaningful patterns in a network result primarily from the condition of the weights. To think of traces in language as *weights* helps us to conceive of them not as something ephemeral, but as something actual, albeit an actuality that is sparse.

Similarly, Derrida's concept of *différance* can be used to describe the *dynamics* of complex neural networks. The analogy works in the following way. If an ensemble of neurons (whether real or artificial) generates a pattern of activity, traces of the activity reverberate through the network. When there are loops in the network, these traces are reflected back after a certain propagation delay (deferral), and alter (make different) the activity that produced them in the first place. Since complex systems always contain loops and feedback, delayed self-altering will be one of the network's characteristics. This characteristic has much in common with the notion of *différance* – a concept that indicates difference and deference, that is suspended between the passive and active modes, and that has both spatial and temporal components (Derrida 1982: 1–27). According to the post-structural 'logic' of trace and *différance*, no word in language (or neuron in the brain) has any significance by itself. Meaning is determined by the dynamic relationships between the components of the system. In the same way, no node in a neural network has any significance by itself – this is the central implication of the notion of distributed representation. Significance is derived from patterns of activity involving many units, patterns that result from a dynamic interaction between large numbers of weights.

Turning to practical neural networks being used at present to solve problems (mainly in the field of pattern recognition), some qualifications have to be made. Practical networks are generally designed to perform specific tasks. They have a limited number of neurons and usually a limited pattern of interconnections. Limits are also placed on the values of the weights and the transfer functions of the neurons. Furthermore, a network is designed for a specific problem, and the weights are usually only altered during a learning phase. They are, generally speaking, not flexible enough to address wide-ranging problems. In this sense, neural networks are structural rather than post-structural, and can be described quite adequately in Saussurian terms. Post-structural concepts do become important, however, should we want to stretch the capabilities of present networks, especially in the context of AI. Networks more successful at mimicking human behaviour will have to be much more flexible. They should be able to innovate under novel conditions, i.e. they will have to be able to move beyond predetermined limits. Towards these ends, insights gained from post-structuralism may contribute enormously.

A detailed analysis of self-organisation and of the representation of information in complex systems will follow. Before that, as a kind of interlude, I will briefly look at the arguments of someone who is incapable of seeing anything useful in the post-structural approach: John Searle.

4   John Searle befuddles

Before we continue our development of a postmodern perspective on complexity, I will examine the arguments of a thinker who explicitly rejects such an approach. John Searle is perhaps not purely an analytical philosopher, but it will become clear from his arguments that he follows a strictly rule-based approach to complex systems like language and the brain. From within such a framework it is possible, he believes, to dismiss Derrida on the one hand, and demolish the project of artificial intelligence on the other.

In 1980 Searle published an article in the prestigious journal *Behavioral and Brain Sciences*, under the title 'Minds, Brains, and Programs'. Intending to supply a knock-down argument against any position which assumes that a computer running a program can ever be said to think, the article triggered a debate that has continued unabated ever since. As the journal practises 'open peer commentary', the original article was accompanied by twenty-eight critiques, followed by more in subsequent issues, all answered by Searle with great confidence (Searle 1982, 1985). The debate was not only continued in other journals (P.M. Churchland and P.S. Churchland 1990; Denning 1990; Harnad 1989; Rapaport 1986) and books (Bierwisch 1990; Münch 1990; Penrose 1989), but the original article was included in many anthologies of articles important for cognitive science and artificial intelligence (Haugeland 1981; Hofstadter and Dennett 1982). After a series of lectures on the BBC, published as *Minds, Brains and Science* (Searle 1984), the debate spilled over into the popular press, where it still surfaces regularly. Despite countless telling counter-arguments, Searle maintains his position with serene confidence (Searle 1990).

Why has this text received so much attention? The subject of intelligent computers – or artificial intelligence (AI) – is certainly generating a great deal of interest. Apart from being a strong and well-supported scientific research programme, it has caught public attention mainly as a result of a few good popular books (Hofstadter 1980; Penrose 1989 – the first 'for', the second 'against'). AI also has a great deal of philosophical interest. Its failure or success has important implications for our understanding of complex systems (including human beings) and how they work. It also fits into a general philosophical tradition and strategy – one that goes by the generic name of 'analytical'. The status of a large number of theories, especially ones concerning brains and minds, would be influenced radically should a conclusive answer to the problem of AI be found. Searle's paper thus deals with a contentious and exciting issue.

But why should this specific paper, in a field already swamped with publications, generate so much interest? For all the wrong reasons. Searle does not provide a particularly clear argument, and the subsequent debate does not really illuminate the problem to any greater degree. It is blindly accepted by everyone who wants to dismiss AI, and viciously opposed by AI supporters. My suspicions are awakened by the ease with which the confrontation takes place. This fifteen-year-old saga of accusations and counter-claims has the distinct flavour of a family feud. In my analysis of his position I will attempt to show that Searle is not a major opponent of the artificial intelligentsia, but, rather, that he is one of the clan.

THE CHINESE ROOM

Searle's argument against any strong form of AI takes the form of a *Gedankenexperiment* (Searle 1980: 417–418). He asks us to imagine an English-speaking man who knows absolutely no Chinese, sitting in a room. He is given a bunch of Chinese symbols along with a rule-book that formally describes the Chinese syntax. To him the symbols are meaningless squiggles, but by following the rules he can manipulate them. If he is given a set of symbols from outside, he can generate a new set and give it back. From outside the room it appears as if the person inside can speak Chinese since he responds appropriately to prompts and questions, yet the person inside does not understand a word of Chinese in the way that he does understand English. He is just following a set of formal rules. Since that is exactly what a computer does – follow a set of rules – no computer will have an 'understanding' of what it is doing, and can therefore not be said to think.

The scenario sketched here is one quite familiar to the AI community. It closely resembles the test proposed by the computing pioneer Alan Turing (1950) for establishing whether a machine is intelligent. Basically, the test consists of having an extended conversation with a hidden computer via a terminal. If at the end of the conversation you cannot say whether you talked to a person or a machine, the computer is said to have passed the Turing test. Although the prominence given to linguistic capabilities has been questioned by some – like Harnad (1989), who would like to introduce a robotic version called the Total Turing Test – the Turing test remains a generally accepted benchmark for machine intelligence. Searle claims to have shown conclusively that a computer can pass the Turing test for understanding Chinese, yet it cannot really understand or think. By implication this result discredits the Turing test as an adequate test for intelligence (Searle 1980: 419).

Up to this point Searle seems to provide a clear and concise argument that could provide the starting-point for an interesting discussion. However, he immediately anticipates a number of critical replies, and defends his conclusions against them. This leads him into troubled waters, a fact that becomes apparent when we examine some of these replies, and Searle's responses, closely:

- *The systems reply* (419): Saying that the man doing the manipulation cannot be said to understand Chinese is like saying the central processor of a computer cannot understand. This ignores the all-important rule-book (or program). The whole system together – man, rule-book and symbols – can be said to understand Chinese, and therefore a computer plus its program can also. To this Searle responds by claiming that there is nothing that prevents the man from memorising the rule-book. He will then contain the whole system, yet still not understand what he is doing by following the rules.
- *The robot reply* (420): Suppose the Chinese program forms part of a system controlling a robot that not only gives appropriate answers, but also performs the appropriate actions. Such a robot would have genuine understanding. Searle responds by saying that the controlling program makes no distinction between inputs coming from the robot's various 'perceptual apparatus'. To the program, all information consists merely of symbols that are manipulated formally, and this does not imply any understanding.
- *The brain simulator reply* (420–421): Suppose the working of a brain (that can speak Chinese) is simulated to such detail that all the functional processes going on inside it are reflected. Such a simulation must be able to understand Chinese, otherwise one would be forced to deny that the original Chinese speaker, the one whose brain is being simulated, understands anything he says. Searle remains undaunted. This simulation, he claims, can be implemented by someone operating an elaborate system of pipes and valves, where the pipes and valves represent the structure of the brain, right down to the level of neurons and synapses. He continues:

  Now where is the understanding in this system? It takes Chinese as input, it simulates the formal structure of the synapses of the Chinese brain, and it gives Chinese as output. But the man certainly doesn't understand Chinese, and neither do the water pipes, and if we are tempted to adopt what I think is the absurd view that somehow the conjunction of man and water pipes understands, remember that in principle the man can internalize the formal structure of the water pipes and do all the 'neuron firings' in his imagination. The problem with the brain simulator is that it is simulating the *wrong things* about the brain. As long as it simulates only the formal structure of the sequence of neuron firings at the synapses, it won't have simulated what matters about the brain, namely its *causal properties, its ability to produce intentional states.* And that the formal properties are not sufficient for the causal properties is shown by the water pipe example: we can have all the formal properties carved off from the relevant neuro-biological causal properties.

(421; my emphases)

In the reaction to Searle's article, there are a large number of other critiques, but he uses the answers to these three (the systems reply, the robot reply and the brain simulator reply) to form the basis of his defence against them all. Most counter-arguments are reduced to one of these types, and then his canned answer to that type of reply is offered as refutation. The ease with which it is done is a result of the fact that Searle's claims are tautologous, and that they can therefore be used to counter any claim what-soever, or to bolster any argument against strong AI. The tautologies become clear in the final pages of Searle's text. He concludes his argument by asking what it is that brains have that enable them to understand and think? How do they differ from programs? Searle's answer is that they have Intentionality: '[C]ertain brain processes are sufficient for intentionality. Instantiating a computer program is never by itself a sufficient condition for intentionality' (417). What, may one ask, is 'Intentionality'? In the Chinese Room article he provides no definition, but in his book entitled *Intentionality* (Searle 1983), where, incidentally, the word is always capitalised, one finds this: 'Intentionality is that property of mental states and events by which they are directed at or about or of objects and states of affairs in the world' (1). His formulation in the following passage is revealing:

Intentionality is not an ontological problem at all. What, for example, is a belief really? . . .

A belief is a propositional content in a certain psychological mode, its mode determines a mind-to-world direction of fit, and its propositional content determines a set of conditions of satisfaction. Intentional states have to be characterized in Intentional terms if we are not to lose sight of their intrinsic Intentionality. But if the question is 'What is the mode of existence of belief and other Intentional states?' then from everything we currently know about how the world works the answer is: Intentional states are both caused by and realized in the structure of the brain.

(14, 15)

'Intentional states have to be characterized in Intentional terms if we are not to lose sight of their intrinsic Intentionality.' This claim is either tautolo-gous, or just plain nonsense. I cannot see in what sense a computer program that has to open, say, a valve under certain conditions is less 'about' some-thing in the world than a belief in the brain is, unless there is something mystic to the substance of the brain. Such a hypothesis would seem to be substantiated by the following statement from the Chinese Room paper: 'Stones, toilet paper, wind, and water pipes [all materials from which computing devices could be constructed] are the wrong kind of stuff to have intentionality in the first place – only something that has the same causal powers as the brain can have intentionality' (Searle 1980: 423). If you cut out the metaphysics, you end up with a gross circularity: brains differ from programs because brains have Intentionality and programs do not. What is Intentionality? Intentionality is that which distinguishes brains from programs.

This is not the end of the circles and contradictions. On the last page of the Chinese Room paper we find the following: ' "Could a machine think?" My own view is that only machines could think, and indeed only very special kinds of machines, namely brains and machines that had the same causal powers as brains' (424). What are these 'causal powers', and where do they come from? Searle gives us no clues, but continues: 'Of course the brain is a digital computer. Since everything is a digital computer, brains are too' (424). That after claiming in the 'brain simulator reply' (420) that no matter how accurately a brain is simulated, the simulation remains a formal system, and is therefore incapable of Intentionality! I give up. The most plausible conclusion to be drawn from all this seems to be that only digital computers can understand Chinese, and that any person who has learnt it cannot.[1]

Why, then, has this flapdoodle sustained a lively debate for nearly two decades? Because, I claim, Searle is a closet member of the AI fraternity. He comes up with an argument in such familiar terms that they can all have a jolly good time in shooting it down. The confrontation takes place with such ease because they all share a set of basic premises. These *premises* are what should be scrutinised closely.

THE FRAMEWORK OF THE CHINESE ROOM

Before analysing Searle's implicit assumptions, I want to return to the claim that his argument has a metaphysical flavour. In his discussion of Searle's argument, Richard Rorty brings the whole issue into an interesting perspective (Searle 1980: 445–446). Searle, he says, goes about his argument in exactly the same way as would a fundamentalist Catholic defending transubstantiation:

> Suppose a demythologizing Tillichian theologian urges that we think of the Eucharist not in terms of substantial change, but rather in terms of significance in the lives of the faithful. The defender of orthodoxy will reply that the 'natural/supernatural distinction cannot be just in the eye of the beholder but must be intrinsic; otherwise it would be up to any beholder to treat anything as supernatural.'
>
> (445)

Just as the orthodox theologian knows in advance what would distinguish natural from supernatural, and what the special 'causal powers' of the supernatural are, Searle knows in advance that a computational process cannot be a cognitive state because it cannot have the same 'causal powers'.

In his reply to Rorty, Searle (453) rejects the parallel as 'totally irrelevant', since Rorty merely supplies an argument with similar form. The truth of the argument depends on the truth of the premises, and Searle then immediately states what he takes to be his own premises: 'They are such things as that people have mental states such as beliefs, desires and visual experiences, that they also have brains, and that their mental states are causally the products of the operation of their brains' (453). I assume that these premises are supposed to be taken as 'common sense', and that nobody in their right mind would dispute them, because Searle does not argue for them at all. Staying *within* the framework of his argument, one could claim that mixing these premises with a few dollops of fresh Intentionality would produce all Searle's claims in a trivial way, but perhaps it is time to question the frame itself. These 'common sense' premises – whether we accept them or not – obscure another set of premises. These are never stated explicitly, but are central to the whole *Gedankenexperiment*. They concern the nature of language.

The object in the Chinese Room on which Searle's whole argument turns is the book containing the rules for manipulating the symbols. Although some commentators do comment on the probable size and complexity of such a rule-book, there does not seem to be much concern about the *possibility* of such a book. Searle, not daunted by practicalities, blankly states its existence. This statement points to at least three important assumptions implicit in Searle's theory of language.

In the first place, he assumes that a formal grammar for a natural language can be constructed and presented in the form of a lookup table. The second assumption, closely linked to the first, presupposes a clean split between syntax and semantics. This point Searle states explicitly: 'The rules specify the manipulation of the symbols purely formally, in terms of their syntax not their semantics' (Searle 1984: 32). Searle's concept of 'rule' therefore appears to be identical to the way in which Chomsky uses it in his early formulations, namely in the sense of *production* rule (Chomsky 1957).

Searle's third assumption concerns the nature of *meaning*. In *Speech Acts* he rejects the notion of 'meaning is use' as too vague (Searle 1969: 146). This is replaced by a theory of 'meaning as Intention' (Searle 1983: 160). We have already encountered the vagueness of his notion of intention. How would it support a theory of meaning? Searle's position is the following: 'Intentionality is precisely that feature of mental states, human or otherwise [*sic*], that enables those states to represent other things' (Searle 1979: 197). Searle supports a representational theory of meaning. This was already apparent in his early works (cf. Searle 1969: Chapter 4), and has been maintained more recently: 'mental states are "symbolic" at least in the sense that they represent objects and states of affairs in the world' (Searle 1985: 743).[2]

What we now see is a conflation of notions concerning language and mind. Neither Searle nor I would object to that. We agree that these issues are inextricably intertwined. However, Searle should be more sensitive to the complexities involved. To reduce the linguistic activity of answering a question to the simple action of 'replace squiggle-squiggle with squoggle-squoggle' (Searle 1984: 32) is a very threadbare way of arguing about what brains and computers can and cannot do. To my mind there is also a contradiction involved in denying dualism – something he accuses his AI adversaries of (Searle 1980: 423) – but maintaining that there is a clean split between syntax and semantics, and *that* after you have claimed that semantics is a characteristic peculiar to the brain, a result of Intentionality.[3]

The most acrimonious confrontations are those between protagonists from the same faction. It should therefore be clear why Searle picked this particular fight, and why the response is so fervent. Both he and his adversaries share a belief in a formal, rule-based theory of language in which the structure of language can be described by pure syntax, and in which meaning is the result of representation. There is no reason why they should not share the same theory of mind. His adversaries have rubbed his nose in this fact time and time again, but he stubbornly refuses to relinquish his idea of Intentionality. By Searle's own lights, Intentionality will remain a metaphysical concept as long as he refuses the possibility of giving it a formal description. If you do not accept his basic characterisation of language, and I do not, the whole *Gedankenexperiment* never even gets going.

Let me state my position regarding the Chinese Room argument clearly: apart from all its internal contradictions and blind spots, the whole argument is irrelevant because it is based on a theory of language that ignores the complexity of language. Searle blandly accepts that complex systems are, on a philosophical level, no different from simple ones. 'Replace squiggle-squiggle with squoggle-squoggle' contains, for him, the basic principles necessary to manipulate language. The rest is mere detail. I am of the opinion that any conclusions drawn from such a simplistic theory will be of little or no help in saying things about the brain or machines.

After looking at Searle's Chinese Room, it should come as no surprise that he is contemptuously dismissive of post-structuralism.

SEARLE'S REJECTION OF POST-STRUCTURALISM

As Searle perceives himself to be the reigning champion of speech-act theory, he saw it as his duty to take Derrida to task when the latter performed a deconstructive reading of Austin. Searle, of course, knew what Austin *actually* meant, and could therefore rectify Derrida's mistakes. In the altercation that developed between the two, it was again apparent that Searle is prone to oversimplification.

One of the contributions made by Austin (1980) in his development of speech-act theory was to argue that the meaning of an utterance depends on the context in which the speech act is performed, where 'context' includes the social conventions pertaining to the act. There existed, however, a need to find some measure of the success, or felicity, of a speech act. The generally accepted solution is to suggest that the success of the act is determined by the congruence of the intentions of the speaker and the given circumstances or context. If they are properly matched, the correct meaning, or illocutionary force, is conveyed, resulting in a successful speech act.

In an important essay entitled 'Signature Event Context', Derrida comes to grips with exactly this point.[4] For him, neither the intention of the speaker, nor the context, is fixed enough to determine the correct meaning of any form of communication. Because any utterance becomes untethered from its origin as soon as the 'tokens' of which it consists – whether these tokens are the sounds uttered by a speaker or words written down – are let loose, so to speak, the intention cannot 'accompany' the linguistic act to control its interpretation. The act of communication is always one of 'dissemination' (Derrida 1988: 2). The context, on the other hand, is also not given objectively. Derrida tries to show 'why a context is never absolutely determinable, or rather, why its determination can never be entirely certain or saturated' (3).

The structural necessity that a sign be repeatable, i.e. that one should be able to use it again and again, in different circumstances, is responsible for the fact that a sign can operate in the radical absence of both sender and receiver (7). Derrida calls this the *iterability* of the sign. This is also part of the reason why Derrida claims that 'writing', rather than 'speaking', is a more appropriate metaphor to use when discussing the basic nature of language. The break with the speaker as 'origin' of meaning, and the absence of any predeterminable receiver, preclude a 'continuous modification of presence' in the process of communication. The sender, the receiver and the message can never be 'present' to each other in order to guarantee the felicity of the speech act. When we interpret a message, we have to do exactly that – interpret. For a sign to be interpretable, it has to be recognisable as that particular sign, and not any other. However, the meaning of what is repeated is never identical. A sign has a history, and this history influences its meaning. Each time the sign is used, it interacts with the other members of the linguistic system, whereby its meaning is shifted, sometimes imperceptibly, sometimes significantly. The notion of iterability describes both the stability of the sign and the dynamics of its meaning, and is closely linked to the notions of trace and *différance*.

Derrida's analysis of language has important implications for our discussion of complexity: it results in 'the disruption, in the last analysis, of the authority of the code as a finite system of rules', as well as 'the radical destruction of any context as the protocol of the code' (8). In sum, it argues against the possibility of a rule-based description of language.

Searle (1977) reacted to Derrida's paper, arguing that Derrida has completely misrepresented Austin's position, that he has confused iterability with a general citationality, and that speech acts remain 'datable singular events in particular historical contexts' (208). Speakers and hearers can understand new things because they are 'masters of the sets of rules we call the rules of language' (208).

To this Derrida responded with a lengthy reply in which he not only argued for his position, but, above all, *demonstrated* it. He showed how, despite his best efforts, Searle cannot prevent his words from shifting their meaning. This was demonstrated by merely quoting (i.e. iterating) Searle's words under circumstances where the context is not determinable. Linking Searle's claims to be the true interpreter of Austin's work with the copyright claim Searle places at the start of his article, Derrida implies that Searle tries to run a closed shop – hence the title *Limited Inc*. He also makes a mocking of the copyright claim accompanying the article by quoting every word of Searle's reply somewhere in his article, including the copyright claim. Through this series of misrepresentations Derrida seems to suggest that no real communication has taken place between them, that the confrontation cannot even be said to have commenced.

The Derrida–Searle altercation has important implications for the Chinese Room argument specifically, and for our discussion of complexity in general. In the first place, it denies that 'Intentionality' can act as a final point of reference for either the meaning of language or the fundamental characteristics of consciousness. Not that Derrida denies the *existence* of intentionality: 'the category of intention will not disappear; it will have its place, but from that place it will no longer be able to govern the entire scene and system of utterance' (Derrida 1988: 18). The notion of Intentionality, which for Searle clearly has metaphysical dimensions, can therefore not be used as a ready-made explanation for the emergent properties of a complex system. The discussion thus confirms Searle's insensitivity to complexity, something of which Derrida is quite aware: 'One shouldn't complicate things for the pleasure of complicating,' he says, 'but one should also never simplify or pretend to be sure of such simplicity where there is none. If things were simple, word would have gotten around' (119).

Should the Chinese Room have any effect on our deliberations? Not much, I think. Continued attacks on, or defences of, Searle's argument will not be of real benefit to anybody. For that the Chinese Room is just too insubstantial. Furthermore, there are fundamental difficulties involved in approaching complex systems with formal models based on production rules. We have no knock-down argument proving either the possibility or the impossibility of machines that can think. That depends on our future success in modelling complex systems – a contingent matter on which the jury is still out. However, I do want to argue that it is unlikely that machines based only on systems of production rules will be able to cope with, for example, natural language. It is, of course, the argument of this book that connectionist networks hold a certain promise in this regard. Patricia and Paul Churchland (1990) feel that these networks are powerful enough to overcome Searle's objections (assuming it still needs to be done), but Searle (1990) sees nothing new in connectionism – a conclusion to be expected, given his old arguments against brain simulations.

Most supporters of connectionism, including the Churchlands, defend their position within the context of theories presently dominant in AI research. The most important of these is a representational theory of meaning. For the Churchlands at least, neural networks still represent the information in a traditional way. I am not suggesting that the connectionist model in its present form is a panacea for all our modelling woes. A lot of work still needs to be done. I do suggest, however, that in the process of doing it, meaningful insights can be gained from the theory of post-structuralism.

I want to conclude with a final objection to Searle's argument and to the way in which he presents it.[5] It is only too easy to make Intentionality the kingpin of all your arguments, but when asked what it is, you find it sufficient to say that it is merely the 'aboutness' of the brain. It is equally facile to reduce language to 'replace squiggle-squiggle with squoggle-squoggle'. Complex issues demand complex descriptions, and a certain humility. Searle fails to acknowledge any intellectual indebtedness and lacks a historical perspective. In a book with the title *Intentionality* he mentions the name of Husserl only once in passing (Searle 1983: 65). Ideas are usually presented as if they have sprung perfect and complete from his forehead. This complacency is also evident from the way he sometimes responds to criticism. When Derrida's two essays discussed above were anthologised (Derrida 1988), Searle refused that his own article be included. When he was recently presented with a volume of critical essays (Burkhardt 1990) after he had promised to react to them, all that the editor received was the 'laconic "Hm" of the "famous man" ' (26). To Derrida's (1988: 29) question 'Where is Searle? Do I know him?' we can perhaps reply: would it make any difference?

5 Problems with representation

Models of complex systems will have to be as complex as the systems themselves. They will also have to emulate these systems' capacity to encode and remember information pertaining to their environment and how to cope with that environment. We have suggested that classical theories of representation do not provide an adequate description of this process. What are the problems presented by representation and why are they important for theory and practice? What are the implications of different methods of representation for our models of complex systems and how do they influence the design and performance of these models? These questions form the framework of this chapter.

A theory of representation is essentially a theory of *meaning*. It is an attempt to explain how the words of our language or the structures in our brain become meaningful, by trying to define relationships between these words or structures and the world. The theory must, however, also explain how these relationships come about. We can use mathematics as an example. The symbols of mathematics have no meaning by themselves. They are provided meaning by means of a definition (e.g. let x stand for the temperature of the water). The symbol is then said to 'represent' that which it stands for. In well-defined problems the relationships between symbols and that which they represent can be specified unambiguously and it is easy to interpret the results. For example, given the laws of Newton, and taking care to use correct representations, the problems of classical mechanics can be solved with great accuracy. If a series of calculations provides you with the answer $t = 10.9$, you only have to know what t represents (a matter of *a priori* definition) in order to interpret the results.

Unfortunately, the ease with which symbols can be made to represent something vanishes when we deal with complex problems, problems for which clear definitions and well-defined borders are less easily found. From the perspective of traditional mathematics, these problems were seen as intractable, but the phenomenal rise in the power of computers has turned attention back to complex issues such as the modelling of natural language, the modelling of human sensory capabilities (e.g. pattern recognition, computer vision), the simulation of higher cognitive processes (reasoning, decision-making) and sophisticated motoric behaviour (robotics). In these cases the process of representation is far from straightforward. How does a word in a language represent something? How do experts represent their knowledge? Does a pattern contain certain explicit features that can be represented in a pattern-recognition machine? The issue is compounded by the fact that with many of these systems, especially living systems, it is not possible to grant an important role to an external designer without very serious metaphysical implications. To make some transcendental principle (like God or Universal Ideas) the first premise of your theory of representation begs too many questions. It is therefore also necessary to explain the process by which the relationships between symbols and the world are *established*. These are the problems faced by those who wish to develop computational models of complex systems, and they are not new. They form part of a long tradition of philosophical reflection on the relationships between language, the mind and the world.

In the context of the computational modeller, it seems as if the problem of representation can be addressed, broadly speaking, in two ways. In the first place we have the rule-based approach of classical computer science and AI. Here there is a basic acceptance of the adequacy of logical calculus – a kind of rationalist approach. In the second place we have the connectionist or neural network approach, which has a more empirical flavour. For both these approaches the problem of representation is the central one (Brooks 1991: 139; Guenthner *et al.* 1986: 39). In the case of neural networks, the problem of representation translates into the following questions: What is the relationship between the structure of the network ('structure' usually refers to the values and connection patterns of the weights) and the phenomena that caused it? How does a network represent the information of the domain it models? Is it possible to analyse the structure of a successful network in order to determine how it solved the problem? How do you use *a priori* knowledge to predetermine the structure of a network, should such information be available? Are rule-based representations and network representations reducible to each other?

These are all issues that have practical significance for the designer and user of neural networks. This chapter will attempt to address them by clarifying those all-important pre-mathematical considerations that determine the framework for any specific model. It will take the form of a critique of the classical notion of representation. This will be followed by an analysis of the notion of distributed representation – as found in connectionist networks. It will be argued that this approach puts the whole notion of representation under pressure. If it can be argued convincingly that connectionism does not rely on a strong theory of representation, this will further emphasise the importance of post-structural theory for our understanding of complex systems. The technical discussion of the problem of representation will therefore be followed by a look at the way in which some postmodern philosophers (specifically Baudrillard and Derrida) deal with it.

TRUE REPRESENTATION

> There is only one language suitable for representing information – whether declarative or procedural – and that is first-order predicate logic. There is only one intelligent way to process information – and that is by applying deductive inference methods.

This statement by Kowalski (quoted in Guenthner *et al.* 1986: 41) epitomises the computer science attitude to the problem of representation. Perhaps one should admire the bravery involved in making such a bold statement, but such blind faith in logic is simplistic. Yet, despite a number of qualifications and reservations, most researchers involved in the modelling of complex systems will implicitly or explicitly support Kowalski's credo. I do not wish to underestimate the importance of logic, but it is also important to realise its limitations. I will attempt to bring these limitations to the fore by analysing a theory of representation that roughly accepts this credo. Such a critique will hopefully provide support for the connectionist approach, an approach that does not take deductive inference and first-order logic as its point of departure.

Functionalism

Two complex systems – the human brain and natural language – are of particular interest. Since they seem to solve (or bypass) the problem of representation, they provide the existence proof that a solution is possible. If these two systems can be modelled successfully, the problem should largely have been solved. Moreover, these two systems seem to be inextricably intertwined – a successful model of one would imply a successful model of the other. That is why most models of the mind are based on – or incorporate – a theory of language. The one we are about to turn to is no exception.

The prevalent theory of the mind in the world of computational modelling is called functionalism. Although not a member of the faith any more, one of the founders of functionalism was Hilary Putnam.

> I may have been the first philosopher to advance the thesis that the computer is the right model for the mind. I gave my form of this doctrine the name 'functionalism', and under this name it has become the dominant view – some say the orthodoxy – in contemporary philosophy of mind.
>
> (Putnam 1988: xi)

The computer metaphor for the mind functions in the following way: a working computer has two components, the machine itself (the hardware) and the programs that are run on the machine (software). The software (which operates on a different logical level) can be transported from one piece of hardware to another and still perform in exactly the same way. A similar relationship is said to hold between the mind and the brain. The brain constitutes the 'hardware' which can run different programs. These programs produce the effects of 'mind'. Just as computer software is not restricted to a specific machine, the mind can likewise be implemented on other pieces of hardware, on condition that they have adequate computing power. This last point needs elaboration.

According to functionalism, a certain physical state of the machine (the brain) *realises* a certain functional state. This provides us with two *independent* descriptions of the same event: one on the physical level, and one on the mental level (Sterelny 1990: 5). The mind is implemented in the brain, but can in principle also be implemented on other machines with adequate computing power. The digital computer, or to be more specific, the Turing machine, functionalists claim, could have adequate power.

Granting the basic premises of functionalism, the theory raises two questions. The first one concerns the adequacy of a physical system to implement functional states. Does a bucket of water qualify? It is certainly complex enough to implement a myriad of states. In order to disqualify systems like these, Sterelny (1990: 10) provides two criteria for adequate physical systems:

- They are designed.
- They have a teleological explanation.

Sterelny side-steps the first criterion by opting for evolution as the designer, but forgets that evolution also produced the spider-web and countless other 'mindless' systems. I think the statement has to be taken at face value: accepting the theory of functionalism implies the existence of an independent external designer. I will return to this point. The second criterion is also problematic. Sterelny does not really explain what he means by it, except to state that something like a bucket of water or the solar system does not have a telos, while the brain and the body do. I suspect the concept he omits here is that of 'intention', the same concept used by John Searle (1980) to save his Chinese Room argument. You cannot say what it is, but you recognise it when you find it. Both criteria have a metaphysical flavour that should be acknowledged by the proponents of functionalism.

The second question that functionalism raises concerns the relationship between the two independent descriptions of the same physical event. What gives a certain physical state a certain meaning? This question will be addressed in the next section.

The language of thought

The functional states of a physical system can only be given meaning if they *stand for* something. Functionalism is meaningless without representation. The grammatical structure of language represents semantic content and the neurological states of the brain represent certain mental states. In both examples, representation is responsible for establishing a link between the states of the system and conceptual meaning.

There can be no informational sensitivity without representation. There can be no flexible and adaptive response to the world without representation. To learn about the world, and to use what we learn to act in new ways, we must be able to represent the world, our goals and options. Furthermore we must make appropriate inferences from these representations.

(Sterelny 1990: 21)

Representation is the process whereby the two levels of description – the symbol and its meaning – are related. How this happens, and how the different representations interact, have to be spelt out by a theory of representation. Although there are a number of variations on it, the core of a generally accepted theory of representation has been worked out by Jerry Fodor (1975, 1981), building on the linguistic theories of Noam Chomsky (1957, 1972) and their psychological implications (e.g. Chomsky 1980). I will return to some of the variations, but first we have to summarise the basic characteristics of representation *à la* Fodor.

The fundamental proposition of Fodor's model is that we think in a special *inner* language, often referred to as 'mentalese' (Fodor 1975). Mentalese is not an equivalent of the language we speak (e.g. French or German), but prior to it. Our capacity for mentalese is not something we acquire or learn, it is an innate capacity of our brains. Like other languages, mentalese is medium-independent. Thus, there are no written or spoken words in our heads; the language is implemented in our neural structure.

Thoughts share two important characteristics with language. In the first place, language is *productive* – the length of any sentence can be increased without the meaning of the sentence collapsing. In the second place, language is *structured* – it has a grammar that allows us to make inferences about linguistic elements previously unrelated. If A and B share a specific relationship to C, language allows us to infer a relationship between A and B without empirical verification. Similarly, thoughts can be concatenated indefinitely and they can be used to make systematic inferences. From this it follows, claims Fodor, that mentalese must share with language that one thing that best explains productivity and structure: a formal syntax.[1] This conclusion is summarised by Sterelny (1990: 26) in the following way:

For this model, and any based on it, requires an agent to represent the world as it is and as it might be, and to draw appropriate inferences from that representation. Fodor argues that the agent must have a language-like symbol system, for she can represent indefinitely many and indefinitely complex actual and possible states of her environment. She could not have this capacity without an appropriate means of representation, a language of thought.

This rough outline of the language-of-thought hypothesis will gain some depth if we look at a more formal explication proposed by Cummins (see

Cummins 1991; Morris 1991, 1992). It is once again a computational model of cognition, 'very much in the mould of classical AI' (Morris 1991: 2). The model is summarised in what Cummins calls 'the Tower Bridge picture' (see Figure 5.1). In this picture, the lower arrow indicates the *implementation* level and the higher one the *interpretation* of that level. The symbols would then mean the following: *i* and *o* are respectively the input and output states of the physical system; *g* represents a function that corresponds to some causal law that transforms *i* into *o* at the implementation level; *I* is the interpretation function whereby *i* and *o* are assigned 'content'; and *f* is a function that transforms input content to output content. According to Morris (1991: 3, 4) this model works if and only if the following holds:

(i)   The inputs and outputs have content. This condition stipulates that there must be representation. The states of the system, *i* and *o* must stand for something.

(ii)   At the interpretation level there is an intelligible rule which takes one from input content to output content. This condition specifies the nature of *f*. By stipulating that *f* must be 'an intelligible rule' the kinds of explanation that will be accepted at the 'mental' level are confined to rule-based explanations that can be spelt out. Morris (1991: 4) claims that this is the basic condition since 'we don't qualify as having isolated a single process until we have formulated a rule or function that takes us from one kind of content to another'. The model cannot work without representation since the top level cannot be abandoned.

(iii)   At the implementation level the inputs and outputs are individuated non-semantically (without reference to content), and

(iv)   there is a non-semantic causal law which explains how those outputs are generated from those inputs in that system.

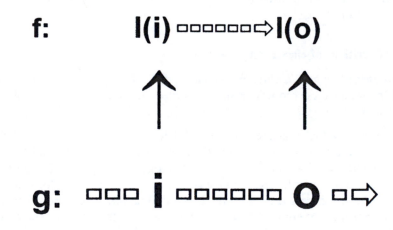

Figure 5.1 The Tower Bridge picture

Condition (iv) specifies the nature of g – a causal law – and together with condition (iii) confirms the complete independence of the implementation (syntactic) and interpretation (semantic) levels. This implies that I cannot be an effect of the physical system itself.

Two further characteristics of this model have to be mentioned. In the first place the model works synchronically. It is committed to an ahistorical notion of representation (Morris 1991: 6). In the second place, the semantic level is logically *prior* to the syntactic level. A definition of what would constitute a 'proper' semantic interpretation (Morris 1991: 7) claims that

$$g(x) = y \text{ if and only if } f[I(x)] = I(y).$$

The claim made by this definition is that the implementation is a *simulation* of the true process that happens at the semantic level. These two characteristics, I feel, are particularly revealing of the embedded metaphysical loyalties of the theory, not only to a kind of Cartesian dualism, but also to an abstract, ahistorical idealism. Morris (1991: 17–19) argues that this formalisation is an adequate description of Fodor's theory of representation.

This concludes the thumbnail sketch of the classical theory of representation. One could perhaps add that the theory is thoroughly modernist in its claim that symbols have abstract, non-contingent meaning. My evaluation and critique of it will emerge in the discussion of connectionist models. The classical theory of representation supplies us with a well-constructed and coherent model for implementing formal systems (i.e. systems that can be given a complete description in terms of predicate logic) computationally, but it is inadequate for the description of complex systems such as natural language and the human brain. Before turning to the connectionist model, I will examine a number of objections to the classical theory of representation coming from one of its first exponents: Hilary Putnam.

Putnam's critique of classical representation

In *Representation and Reality*, Hilary Putnam (1988) argues against his original functionalist position. The main problem he identifies is the role of representation:

> ... given the fact that the key ideas of Chomsky's theorizing are (1) the idea of Linguistic Universals, (2) the Innateness Hypothesis, and (3) the recent idea of modularity, the form that one can expect a Chomskian theory of the semantic level to take is relatively clear (and Fodor's theory does take the expected form), even if the details can take various shapes. A Chomskian theory of the semantic level will say that there are 'semantic representations' in the mind/brain; that these are innate and

universal; and that all our concepts are decomposable into such semantic representations. This is the theory I hope to destroy.

(5)

The Fodor/Chomsky model of representation is what Putnam calls the most recent form of 'mentalism'. The appeal of the theory lies in the way in which it simply identifies belief–desire psychology (or folk psychology) with computational modelling. Mentalism, he says, 'is just the latest form taken by a more general tendency in the history of thought, the tendency to think of concepts as scientifically describable ("psychological real") entities in the mind or brain' (7). Putnam claims that the tendency is entirely misguided.

Although he does not really provide useful alternative suggestions (as Goodman [1991] points out), Putnam does have three strong arguments against mentalism, to which I will add a fourth.

(i) *Meaning is holistic.* The first argument against mentalist representation claims that there is not only one relationship between a symbol and the thing it refers to, but many. Meaning is generated by the activity of an ensemble, not by a soloist. The term 'holistic' does not carry a lot of baggage here (it has nothing to do with organically grown alfalfa sprouts); it merely points to the fact that we are faced with a network of relationships when dealing with meaning. Such a holistic approach has to counter two theoretical tendencies.

In the first place, holism is opposed to positivism. A positivistic tendency would want to reduce meaning to definitions formulated in an 'epistemologically more primitive' language (Putnam 1988: 8), whose components can be given meaning in an unambiguous way (in sensational, or at least observable, terms). In the second place, holism counters the tendency to fix the meaning of terms by means of *definition* since 'most terms *cannot* be defined – or, at least, cannot be defined if by a "definition" one means something that is fixed once and for all, something that absolutely captures the meaning of the term' (9).

The argument from holism argues against representation in the first place not because it is an abstraction, but because it is an oversimplification. It embodies a kind of idealistic optimism that we will get things right in the end without getting our hands dirty in the complex struggles and interactions of contingency.

(ii) *Meaning is in part a normative notion.* The argument followed here is not the post-structural one that claims meaning is both produced and distorted by complex relationships – which would include relations of power. Putnam's claim is simply that since the meaning of a term cannot be defined in terms of some basic or physicalist concept that has bottomed out, there are always elements of belief involved. Most of us have not seen an electron, either directly or indirectly, and even those who claim to have evidence of its existence have to submit their claims within a certain theoretical framework. Our understanding of what an electron is, is based on a system of shared beliefs, and since we do not all have the same degree of knowledge concerning electrons, these beliefs differ.

If the symbols in a system had only one correct and complete meaning, communication would break down if that essence was missed. In normal, successful communication, we do not have to insist on essences, but rather give each other the benefit of the doubt. This is sometimes known as the 'principle of charity'. All interpretation depends on charity, because 'we always have to discount at least *some* differences in belief when we interpret' (13).

(iii) *Meaning depends on the environment.* This argument is primarily aimed at Fodor's Innateness Hypothesis and claims that our environment has produced notions which could not have been foreseen by evolution 30,000 years ago (15). Moreover, our complex interactions with the environment must play a role in the establishment of meaning, and changing our different environments would affect the generation of meaning, irrespective of any hypothesis of innateness. We are not coherent, abstract subjects *experiencing* our world; we are *produced* by our world, we change it and we are changed by it.

(iv) *Meaning is a historical concept.* Although Putnam does not include the temporal aspects of meaning as a separate argument, it forms part of all three of the above arguments. At this stage it bears repetition that the states of a complex system are determined not only by external circumstances, but also by the *history* of the system. These aspects interact in a non-linear, recursive way that can by no stretch of the imagination be described in terms of first-order predicate logic.

Putnam does not really indicate how these objections can be overcome, but they will have to be taken seriously. It is clear that 'classical' representation is not an adequate model for explaining how a complex system stores and uses information. If an alternative is to be suggested, it will have to take into account the four characteristics of meaning discussed above. In what follows it will be argued that a certain interpretation of connectionism may fare somewhat better in this respect.

CONNECTIONISM

Basic connectionist theory will not be repeated here (see Chapter 2 for an introduction), but let us briefly summarise the most important characteristics of neural networks before we turn to how they 'represent' information.

Neural network characteristics

A neural network consists of a large collection of interconnected nodes or 'neurons'. Each neuron receives inputs from many others. Every connection has a certain 'strength' associated with it, called the 'weight' of that connection. These weights have real values that can be either positive (excitatory), negative (inhibitory) or zero (implying that the two respective neurons are not connected). The neurons themselves are very simple computational units. They calculate the sum of their weighted inputs and pass this value through a non-linear transfer function. This function usually has a sigmoidal shape.

Some of the neurons in the network serve as input units that receive information from outside. Similarly, some neurons serve as output units where the result of the network's calculations can be found. In simple network structures, like the multi-layer perceptron or back-propagation network, the neurons are arranged in layers. One would then have an input layer, some in-between layers (usually called 'hidden layers') and an output layer. If an input is presented to the network, it will percolate through the network and generate an output. Since the neurons themselves are all essentially similar, the transformation performed by the network is determined by the values of the weights.

How are these weights determined? The network is basically trained to perform certain tasks by showing it examples. If the network has to perform a classification task, e.g. classifying trees, it is shown examples of trees and of things that can be confused with trees. During a learning phase each presentation (which takes the form of an array of numerical values, say the intensities of each co-ordinate on a retina, or the pixel values of each co-ordinate on a screen or photograph) is accompanied by the correct output value for that input. The network then automatically adjusts the values of the weights to minimise the discrepancy between the input and the output. These presentations are continued until the network converges on a set of weight values that enables the network to distinguish between the various examples of trees and non-trees. If the training examples were adequate, the network should also be able to generalise its classification to examples of trees it has not seen before.

The neural network most often applied in practice – the multi-layer perceptron trained with the back-propagation algorithm – is a simple network which has all the basic characteristics mentioned above.

Storage and manipulation of data in neural networks

From the discussion above it should be clear that the difference between any two networks would mainly be determined by the values of the weights.[2] The characteristics of any specific network is a result of the distribution of these values. How these weights encode information from the external world depends, for one thing, on the relationship between the number of weights and the type and amount of information the network is presented with. This is an important issue which will be discussed in more detail by looking at three kinds of networks.

The first network to be considered is one in which the nodes of the network stand for specific concepts and the weights for the relationships between them. A simple example would be to make particular nodes stand for members of a group of people. If two people are related, the connection between them is positive, if not, negative. Here we have an automatic relative-recogniser. Activate any node, and all nodes representing relatives will become active. This kind of network is quite well known from traditional AI and is called a semantic network. Nodes and connections have specific interpretations, and since they 'stand for' something, the traditional theory of local representation is used.

The second kind of network is one in which the necessity of a relationship between a certain node and a specific concept is rejected. The example in this case can be a fairly simple pattern-recognition network like a multilayer perceptron that has to recognise trees. Such a network will have a large amount of neurons in the hidden layer – at least of the same order of magnitude as the input layer – of which each one is connected to every input node. The information fed into the network is therefore distributed over all the hidden neurons with the result that none of the neurons stand for anything specific. This also follows from the fact that the amount of hidden neurons necessary to solve a certain problem can vary quite considerably. If a network with 120 hidden neurons has a performance comparable to a network with 100, it does not mean that 20 specific aspects of the problem are not considered by the smaller network, it merely means that the information is now spread over 20 fewer units, with perhaps a slight degradation in the performance of the network.

In this kind of network neither the nodes nor the weights have specific interpretations. The encoded information is not representations of coherent concepts. The representation is often referred to as being 'sub-symbolic' or as encoding 'micro-features' (e.g. Rumelhart and McClelland 1986). No weight has any meaning on its own. Furthermore, all the weights participate each time the network is presented with a pattern. This process of encoding is called 'distributed representation'. The characteristics and importance of distributed representation, as well as the ways in which it links with postmodern theory, will be discussed in some detail later in the chapter, but before that is done, a third kind of network has to be introduced.

For the third alternative, consider the multi-layer perceptron from the last but one paragraph, but reduce the number of hidden neurons to the absolute minimum that will still be able to recognise all the training patterns. This network now develops two interesting characteristics. In the first place, when looking at the distribution of weight values, it becomes apparent that the weights tend towards having either highly positive or highly negative values.

In the second place, when any input pattern is presented, the hidden nodes tend to switch either hard on or hard off. In these networks (to which I refer as 'minimal networks'), the hidden nodes begin to encode specific features of the input pattern; they begin to stand for something specific. Since the weights are either strongly excitatory ('yes') or strongly inhibitory ('no'), they begin to encode logical relationships between nodes representing specific concepts. The implications are clear: despite the fact that we are working with a neural network that is trained in the normal way, we are forcing it to use a kind of local representation by removing all the redundancy in the network.

It is of course not possible to define clear boundaries between these different kinds of networks, since the amount of distributedness will depend on the complexity of the problem. For one problem 50 hidden nodes may implement a high level of distributedness, whereas for a more complex problem, it may only constitute a minimal network. The important point to grasp at this stage is that one cannot talk about distributed representation when using a small network that only encodes logical relationships between units that are either on or off. On the other hand, there is also a serious problem with networks that have too many neurons. When a network is too powerful, it overfits the training data and then generalises poorly. This problem will be tackled when we examine some practical implications of these ideas, but first we should give a closer characterisation of distributed representation.

Distributed representation

In this section I wish to deal with three characteristics of neural networks that are directly related to their distributedness, as well as with three critiques of distributed representation. These should serve to clarify our understanding of the concept.

The first important characteristic is the way in which distributed networks implicitly deal with complexity. In the process of solving a complex problem by using a network, it is not necessary to have an explicit theory about the structure of the problem. In conventional computational problem-solving such a theory is explicitly required in order to construct an algorithm that can be programmed. The construction of a theory therefore precedes all other activities. When dealing with complex systems, however, it can be extremely difficult, if not impossible, to construct such a theory since a large number of factors can interact in complex, non-linear ways. Theory construction under such circumstances involves large-scale reduction of complexity with a high risk of ending up with an abstraction that provides an inadequate model of the system. Since a neural network implicitly encodes the relationships between large amounts of factors in a non-linear, distributed way, the need for a complete and explicit theory falls away. When a network is large enough, it will have enough redundancy to be able to encode all these factors simultaneously. Under practical circumstances the problem is reduced to finding an adequate way of *presenting* the information to the network (an aspect which will receive attention in the next section).

This leads us to an extremely important point: the network used as model for a complex system will have to have the same level of complexity as the system itself. It will therefore be just as difficult to construct a theory of what the network is doing as it would be to construct a theory of what the system is doing. If certain general principles exist that can assist in describing the behaviour of the system, they could possibly be found by analysing the behaviour of the network. However, if the system is truly complex, a network of equal complexity may be the simplest adequate model of such a system, which means that it would be just as difficult to analyse as the system itself. This has serious methodological implications for scientists working with complex systems. A model which reduces the complexity may be easier to implement, and may even provide a number of economical descriptions of the system, but the price paid for this should be considered carefully.

The second characteristic of distributed networks concerns their ability to generalise their solutions. After they have been trained to perform a specific task, they should also be able to deal with new inputs that are related to, but not identical to, the training examples. Since the new inputs will share some, but not all, of the features of the training examples, the training examples cannot be encoded in a fixed or fully constrained representation using specific nodes in the network. In a truly distributed representation, all the nodes, with their associated weights, participate in all the examples. This means that at all times, the maximum amount of information is available at all nodes. Since a local representation is only possible after a process of abstraction – irrespective of whether this abstraction is the result of an *a priori* theory or of the constrained working of a minimal network – the ability of such representations to generalise will decrease as the level of abstraction increases. If only a few explicit features can be considered at any time, any example that does not share these features cannot be considered. For effective classification of complex examples – where a large number of micro-features have to be considered – an adequate distributed representation is a prerequisite.

A third important characteristic of distributed representation concerns the robustness of this approach. When a specific concept or feature is encoded by a *specific* neuron, that concept or feature would be lost should that specific neuron be damaged. However, when the representation is distributed, no specific feature of the network is tied to any specific neuron. Should neurons be damaged, it would degrade the overall operation of the network only slightly. The more distributed the network, the more graceful the degradation.[3] Robustness may be less important to a system that has to deal with idealised abstractions, but it is vital for a system that has to deal with the contingencies of the real world.

Connectionism has received much criticism, especially from the proponents of folk psychology and classical representation. These critiques are often flawed, specifically because the notion of distributed representation is either ignored or misunderstood. Fodor and Pylyshyn (1988) use a semantic net as their example of a neural network, and Clapin (1991) equates a neural network with the CPU in a classical Von Neumann machine! In the following paragraphs I will discuss a number of criticisms which are at least sensitive to the nature of distributed representation. They are taken from Sterelny (1990: 187–189), who is defending a 'language of thought' kind of representational theory. If one shifts the theoretical perspective, many of the critiques against distributed representation actually point to advantages.[4]

A first criticism concerns the status of the weights. For Sterelny, the 'relationship between distributed representations and the micro-features that compose them is deeply problematic' (188). When we define a concept in terms of a cluster of sub-concepts – e.g. when we define 'lemon' by the cluster {fruit, tart, yellow, . . . } – 'we have returned to a theory of the componential analysis of concepts, . . . a theory that has desperate and unsolved problems' (188). Coupled to this, Sterelny has problems with the functions of the weights:

> There is no distinction drawable, even in principle, between functional and non-functional connections. A positive linkage between two nodes in a distributed network might mean a constitutive link (e.g. catlike, in a network for tiger); a nomic one (carnivore, in the same network); an accidental, inductive one (asian, in the same network), or a merely associative one (in my case, a particular football team that play in black and orange).
>
> (189)

It is clear that the notion of 'micro-feature' becomes misleading here. The weights are given specific interpretations with ideational content. In principle, Sterelny is still working with a semantic network. In a truly distributed representation, the informational content of any specific weight is the result of such a dispersed process that it cannot be said to constitute anything specific. There are definitely not different kinds of weights (nomic, constitutive, inductive, etc.).

It is also a misunderstanding of the nature of distributed representation to think that it implements concepts or features by using clusters of components. That would merely be a refinement of a system of local representation. Instead of having one set of symbols with specific semantic interpretations, you now have another, perhaps with more symbols. Distributed representation allows you to discard this whole theoretical framework. Instead of working with concepts or clusters of concepts, you work with a system of relationships at a sub-conceptual level that cannot be given, or rather, is not in need of a semantic interpretation at all. I will return to this below.

A second critique concerns the coherence and stability of the representation.

'Distributed representation does not give you an invariant, context-independent representation' (187). Since the initial state of two systems may vary,
they will never be able to represent exactly the same concept. This is of
course only a problem if you think that invariant, context-independent
representations are necessary or should exist. Postmodern or post-structural
theories of meaning deny this by claiming that both synchronic and
diachronic contexts are not only necessary, but constitutive of meaning.
Since there are no theoretical limitations on the amount of information that
can be fed into a network (given that the network has sufficient capacity),
one can include as much of the context as one wishes. Moreover, since the
information is distributed, no explicit distinction between concept and
context has to be made – they are encoded together; context is always
already part of the representation.

The final critique of distributed representation drives our analysis to the
limit. Sterelny claims:

> it is not clear that a distributed representation is a representation for the
> connectionist system at all. . . . Given that the influence of node on node
> is local, given that there is no processor that looks at groups of nodes as a
> whole, it seems that seeing a distributed representation in a network is
> just an outsider's perspective on the system.
>
> (188)

While this causes Sterelny some distress – 'I demand to be told why I should
regard distributed representation as states of the system at all' (188) – we can
breathe a sigh of relief. Adding up the characteristics of distributed representation we have now worked through, it becomes clear that the very notion of
representation has been undermined. A distributed representation is *not* a
representation in the conventional sense of the word. It dispenses with all the
components of a representational system. There are no symbols that 'stand
for' something, there are no grammatical relationships between them, and
the system itself has no need of a semantic level of interpretation at all. We
need neither a central processor nor an outside observer. I will return to the
philosophical importance of this conclusion in the final section of this
chapter, but I first want to take a brief look at two attempts to develop
connectionist models that do not discard the notion of representation.

Two attempts to save representation

Connectionism has made enough of an impact on cognitive science to elicit
a varied number of responses ranging from outright hostility (Fodor and
Pylyshyn 1988) to a very warm welcome (P.M. Churchland 1989). In this
section I want to look at two responses that claim to be sympathetic to
connectionism. The first, by Lloyd (1989), tries to reconcile connectionism
with traditional representational theory, and the second, by the Churchlands,
finds in connectionism a natural ally for the theory of eliminativism.

Lloyd selects the problem of representation as the central one that has to be solved in order to understand the mind. He wants to develop a theory of representation that is both analytic – 'understanding the parts precedes understanding the whole' (Lloyd 1989: 8) – and reductive – 'a theory that explains how representations are made out of non-representational parts' (11). This kind of theory is already at odds with our understanding of connectionism. Furthermore, Lloyd seems to have a limited understanding of the nature of distributed representation. This is most obvious when he describes the meta-theory that forms the framework of his proposals (11–22). His meta-theory consists of a number of constraints applicable to *any* theory of representation. I wish to argue that these constraints bias his interpretations strongly towards a traditional theory of representation and thereby occlude the more radical implications of distributed representation. Let us examine these constraints briefly.

(i)   Representation has to be accurate. It must be possible to identify the objects being represented (13).

(ii)   Representation must be focused, i.e. it must have a capacity for specificity. It must pick out some objects and sail past others (13–15).

(iii)   Representation must be 'articulated'. Meaningful representations are composed out of *independently meaningful parts*. 'In sum, atomicity and articulation interlace; representational systems are chunky, with minimal chunks that can be linked to form bigger chunks' (16–17).

(iv)   Representation is asymmetrical. A drawing of a tree represents the tree; the tree does not represent the drawing (17).

(v)   Representation has to have a cognitive role, i.e. it must be able to fulfil the intentional function (17).

(vi)   Representation has to come about through evolutionary processes, i.e. processes that can develop through natural selection (18).

(vii)   Representation must be explained through a reductive theory (19).

Except for constraint number (vi), which is neutral to the argument, and (v), which seems to entail much more than merely a characteristic of representation, none of these constraints are compatible with a truly distributed representation. Since he defines all representations in analytic, atomistic terms, Lloyd's constraints, like Sterelny's critiques discussed in the previous section, prevent him from seeing that distributed representation is really not representation at all, and that this is good news.

The Churchlands, on the other hand, have no problem with the elimination of the semantic level. For them, connectionist models are a godsend. They do, however, cling to representation in the sense that distributed representation still forms *representations*. For them the network constitutes 'an organised "library" of internal representation of various prototypical perceptual situations' (P.M. Churchland 1989: 207), or 'smart look-up tables' operating in high-dimensional spaces (P.S. Churchland and Sejnowksi 1992: 138). What is more, the neurons of the internal layers are seen as 'complex feature detectors' (P.M. Churchland 1989: 123). Although this is a popular interpretation of the role of the hidden layer when neural networks are applied to well-defined problems, it belies an acceptance of the cluster theory of representation discussed in the previous section. The Churchlands are careful to avoid the return to a theory of local representation and argue strongly for the advantages of what they call 'vector coding' (P.S. Churchland and Sejnowski 1992: 163–174), but they stop short of accepting that a fully distributed representation is no longer a representation in any traditional sense of the word.

The situation is also compounded by the prevalent use of state-space descriptions in their analyses. Defining the state of a network by a specific point in state-space creates the impression that the point is somehow unique. The state-space description unfortunately does not indicate the relationships between various parameters, nor does it indicate any relationships between sub-spaces. Furthermore, our geometrical intuition fails when we have to visualise high-dimensional spaces. As is the case with interpreting hidden neurons as feature detectors, state-space descriptions of well-defined dynamical systems can be a useful tool. When we try to describe real complexity, however, state-space diagrams tend to exacerbate a prevalent tendency towards atomism.

Despite their insistence on representation, the Churchlands constitute one of the first voices in the theoretical domain that take connectionism seriously to the extent of making it a central component of their models, and in that respect they deserve some support. However, no stretch of the imagination would make it possible to call their approach 'postmodern'.

In what follows I wish to examine the implications of distributed representation at two levels. On the one hand, I wish to show that thinking about representation in this way has implications for the way in which we use neural networks in practical situations (as classifiers or for pattern recognition). This discussion will focus more on technical issues, but it is included in order to show – not just state – that postmodern approaches do have practical consequences, even where mundane applications are concerned. If you believe this already, and feel that engineering examples may not be interesting enough, you could skip the next section and move on to the discussion of some of the philosophical implications of distributed representation.[5]

THE IMPORTANCE OF DISTRIBUTED REPRESENTATION IN PRACTICAL MODELLING

Before turning specifically to neural networks, something should be said about traditional AI methods like expert systems.[6] Since they work with formal symbols in logical relationships, they employ the conventional methods of local representation. This does not mean that there is anything wrong with them *per se*, it just means that you need a very good formal model of the domain you are describing. Adequate models often employ many *ad hoc* rules to cope with exceptions. The more *ad hoc* rules there are, the more 'distributed' the model becomes. Minimal neural networks, on the other hand, begin to look more like expert systems. There are therefore a range of options between fully local and fully distributed representation. The choice made between the two will, however, strongly influence your approach to the problem, and if my analysis is correct, will also have an effect on the results.

Degrees of distributedness

When we use neural networks, not only the structure of the network, but also the way in which data are presented to the network, affects the degree of distributedness. If the data are algorithmically pre-processed in order to extract or emphasise certain features, specific interpretations are forced on to the data, and the freedom of the network is constrained. This may be inevitable under most circumstances since raw data are often just too cumbersome to handle. But by doing a large amount of data-reduction and pre-processing in order to present a neural net with a handful of features selected by the pre-processing algorithm, one is not using the capabilities of neurocomputing effectively. Once you have a number of features, any classical classification technique would be able to perform the necessary task. A further result of heavy pre-processing is that minimal networks are then often sufficient to do the final classification. These are usually trained to a level where the activation levels of the various neurons are either high or low, i.e. on or off, and the weights in the network tend towards their extreme positive or negative values. The result is that the network eventually consists of a number of logical gates making yes–no decisions, with the equivalent reduction in distributedness.

Unfortunately, small networks solving toy problems are widely used to analyse network behaviour. The reason normally given is that only small networks allow detailed analysis. From our perspective, this argument is a self-fulfilling prophecy: only small nets are analysed because only small nets *can* be analysed; avoid nets with distributed representation because they do not fit into our scheme.[7] A related problem concerns the questionable practice of using simulated data and then handcrafting networks to operate successfully on the data. This does not really advance our knowledge of the capabilities and limitations of neural networks – something that can be done better by examining networks to which the notion of distributed representation applies in a meaningful way.

Since distributedness is not an absolute parameter, but depends on the context and the complexity of the problem, it is not possible to provide objective, quantitative criteria for it. In the absence of quantitative definitions of distributedness, a few qualitative considerations may help us. In the first place, the fuller the interconnections, the closer the network is to being distributed. In this sense, the normal back-propagation network – with full interconnection between layers – would qualify, provided that there are enough neurons in total. A second consideration concerns the number of nodes in the network. Since this would once again be determined by the complexity of the problem being addressed, general principles cannot be given. However, I would suggest that a trained network can be analysed in order to determine whether a large percentage of neurons have moved to a yes–no condition. In such a case the network is probably too small. Since there is an intimate relationship between the input data and the values of the weights, the input also has some bearing on the matter. The third consideration thus has to do with the number of training examples. Using only four input vectors to train a network that has two output conditions[8] will certainly not result in true distributedness. The amount of training examples that would be adequate for a certain problem will be determined by the complexity of that problem. If the problem is very simple, a neural network should not be used.

Generalisation in multi-layer perceptrons

The ability of neural networks to operate successfully on inputs that did not form part of the training set is one of their most important characteristics. Networks are capable of finding common elements in all the training examples belonging to the same class, and will then respond appropriately when these elements are encountered again. Optimising this capability is an important consideration when designing a network.

As far as back-propagation networks are concerned, everybody that has worked with them will confirm the following strategy: do not use a network that is larger than necessary to solve the problem, and do not overtrain it. Under such circumstances the network will build up such an accurate representation of the training set that it will disregard examples in the test set that differ only slightly from the training examples. The consideration to keep the network as small as possible is borne out in practice, but there is clearly a tension here between the conditions for good generalisation and the conditions for distributed representation. This needs careful analysis.

The issue of the size of neural networks is beginning to receive more and more attention.[9] Hirose *et al.* (1991) deal with the amount of hidden units in a network. They assume that the amount of input and output units are fixed, and then develop an algorithm that automatically varies the amount of hidden units. This has to alleviate two problems: the first concerns getting stuck in local minima, and the second concerns not knowing the correct amount of hidden units in advance.

Hirose *et al.*'s algorithm is the following: during the training process the total mean-square error E of the network is monitored. If after an epoch of

100 weight updates E has not decreased by more than 1 per cent, it is assumed that the network either has difficulty in converging, or is stuck in a local minimum, and an extra hidden unit is added. Once the network converges, the process is reversed, and hidden units are removed until the network does not want to converge anymore. The network one-before-last is then selected. (This method is reminiscent of parking your car by going until you hear a crunch, and then six inches less.) The algorithm was tested by looking at the XOR problem (see note 7), and at a network learning to recognise 36 characters, consisting of 8×8 pixels that can only assume the values 0 or 1.

I consider this an example of a blind approach to neurocomputing that must be avoided. At this stage of our knowledge, the difficulties networks run into should be highlighted, not obscured by 'automatic' procedures that embrace all the principles I have argued against in the previous section. At the end of the article (66) Hirose *et al.* state that the issue of generalisation was not considered at all, and although they acknowledge that they ran into difficulties when hidden units were not removed in the correct order (64), they do not reflect on the implications this may have for the way they think about the problem.

Generalisation is certainly the concern of the article by Sietsma and Dow (1991). They started off by accepting the delivered wisdom that there must be as few hidden units as possible. By adding another bit of neurocomputing folklore – that networks with more layers may generalise better – they suggested that long, narrow networks may improve generalisation. This hypothesis was tested by training networks to classify a number of sine waves into three frequency classes. To this they added a fourth class, a default that represented everything not in the first three. With an input layer consisting of 64 units, these networks come much closer to being 'distributed' than the networks – consisting of five neurons – used to solve the XOR problem.

The procedure followed was to train networks and then to prune them of all 'redundant' hidden units in order to create minimal networks. Extra layers could then be inserted, and the various options could be tested for generalisation. The effects of adding noise to the test set as well as to the training examples were also investigated. Their observations are significant:

• *Long, narrow networks generalised poorly.* These networks not only gener-alised worse than their 'parent' networks, but also gave a high error rate when noisy inputs were used (Sietsma and Dow 1991: 75). This result can be understood in the light of our discussions of distributed representa-tion. The concatenation of minimal layers making 'logical' distinctions will move the network even more towards a rule-based framework and thereby drastically decrease the level of 'distributedness'. The more 'icon-ical' the representation in the network, the poorer the generalisation.
• *Adding noise to the training set improved generalisation.* Providing some

'smear' to the input vectors would certainly 'distribute' them more, but the effect of adding noise had another important result: networks trained with noisy inputs could not be pruned to the same extent. Units previously thought not to contribute to the solution now proved to do so (Sietsma and Dow 1991: 73). This serves to underline the central characteristic of distributed representation, i.e. that the values of specific nodes are not significant, but that the information lies in the pattern of weights distributed over the whole network. An increase in the amount of hidden units can therefore lead to improved generalisation (Sietsma and Dow 1991: 68, 78).

The outcome of this investigation of long, narrow networks also has implications for pre-processing. In such networks, the first layers actually perform a kind of feature-extracting similar to many forms of pre-processing. This does not imply that all forms of pre-processing should be avoided; data reduction is often essential. It does, however, force one to consider the effects of pre-processing carefully. It should not remove information that can contribute to a good distributed representation, bearing in mind that such information may not be what we would identify as important when viewing the data from the analytical, algorithmic framework scientists habitually employ.

Improving generalisation

Can the observations made above lead to an improvement in the way neural networks are employed in practice? I argue that changing the general theoretical approach, i.e. seeing distributedness as an advantage, not a liability, could affect network performance. Here are some practical considerations following from this line of thought:

(i)   *Do not overtrain.* Overtraining results in a specific representation of the test set, and not in a distributed representation of the problem area. Overtraining can be prevented by interrupting the training process and monitoring the performance of the network on a separate test set. Alternatively, an adjustment can be made of the criteria for deciding whether a network has converged.

(ii)   *Add noise to the training set.* The effects of noise addition have been discussed, but it should be kept in mind that the addition of noise does not increase the information content of the input data, it just shakes it around a little bit. Adding noise may be helpful under circumstances where the amount of input vectors are limited, otherwise the next consideration is much more important.

(iii)   *Increase the range of input examples.* Input vectors should be as representative as possible. Outliers should most definitely be included. They do not only have the same effect as the addition of noise, but also provide significant information that may enable the network better to partition the feature space.

(iv) *Increase the number of output classes.* This consideration may be the most important of all. Just as in Saussure's system of language, classification categories can be defined closer by providing examples of what they are *not*. The more classes there are that the network can reject, the greater the confidence in the final classification. The addition of one, or even better, a few default classes not only improves generalisation, but also makes the system more robust against variations in environmental conditions (level of background noise, presence or absence of 50 or 60 Hz noise, dynamic range, sensor variations, round-off errors, etc.). The clever selection of default classes (background noise, false classes, system noise, elements common to all examples, etc.) allows you to fine-tune your network without fiddling with its insides. For instance, providing a separate class for an element common to all examples (e.g. background noise) not only provides the network with an extra option, but since it has to build a separate representation of the common element, and distinguish it from the true classes, the representations for the true classes become more robust. An inventive selection of output classes also allows you to do different things with the same data.

(v) *Use real data.* Apart from the fact that the use of simulated data often results in self-answering questions, the use of real data results in the incorporation of several important elements of distributed representation automatically. Noise and variation come for free, and there is less of a temptation to insert a 'grand theory' between the problem and the solution.

(vi) *Consider pre- and post-processing carefully.* Do not pre-process the life out of the data. Rather analyse the output of the network for trends and errors.

Post-processing is an aspect of neural networks that has not received enough attention, and I will therefore conclude this section with a few remarks on the subject. If the input to the network and the network itself are made to be as 'distributed' as possible, this will also affect the nature of the outputs. In the first place, there may now be more output neurons than required for a specified solution. Secondly, less pre-processing, especially less averaging of the input vectors, means that a large number of inputs with a greater distribution have to be processed. Though this may increase the *instantaneous* error rate at the output, with appropriate post-processing, the network will perform better on average.

Appropriate post-processing could include averaging or filtering of the outputs, finding better criteria for a 'good' classification, or the use of the outputs as inputs in a following processing stage. The general maxim seems to be that you should not do at the input of the network what can be done at the output.

REPRESENTATION DECONSTRUCTED

In this section I will turn to some of the philosophical implications of our discussion on representation, specifically to the relationship between a distributed way of thinking and aspects of post-structural theory.[10] Post-structuralism is an important and exciting theoretical approach that challenges many of the central assumptions of conventional approaches to language and science. I wish to argue that a distributed approach to the modelling of complex systems has many affinities with post-structuralism, and that post-structuralism can inform our scientific and technological praxis on vitally important issues. Conversely, practical results achieved in making use of the post-structural approach should testify against the perception that post-structuralism is merely a philosophical diversion with destructive tendencies.

One of the important characteristics of post-structural thought, especially in the work of Jacques Derrida, is the denial of the transparency of language. The idea that the meaning of a word is 'present' when the word presents itself creates the illusion of determinate meaning. This identification of a word with a specific meaning is an instance of what Derrida calls the 'metaphysics of presence'. He argues that there is not a one-to-one correspondence between a word and its meaning. Meaning is the result of an interplay between all the words (or, rather, all the signs) in the system. It is an effect of the dynamics within the system, not of direct relationships between components of the system and objects in the world. This does not deny all relationships between the world and the system. To the contrary, the success of the system depends largely on the effectiveness of the interaction between the system and its environment. What it does deny is that these relationships can be unpacked in determinate terms when we deal with a complex system like language or the brain. Complexity cannot be simplified into direct relationships without losing exactly those capabilities of the system we are interested in – the capabilities that emerge as a result of the non-linear, distributed relationships between the constituents of the system.

Despite the fact that we cannot represent the essence of a complex system in determinate terms, we cannot resist, or perhaps even avoid, the construction of some kind of interpretation of the nature of the system at a given moment. These interpretations, however, are in principle limited. We are always constrained to taking snapshots of the system. These shots are always taken from a certain angle and reveal some aspect of the system at some moment. Nothing prevents us from *attempting* explanations of the system – we can take as many pictures as we want – as long as we realise the limitations of each particular one. Since a complex system is constantly changing, i.e. not in equilibrium, it is also not possible to link a series of pictures together like pieces in a puzzle that fit exactly into their true positions. We can juxtapose, compare, make collages, combine them in sequences that develop a narrative, and thereby, in perhaps a more creative way, develop our understanding of the system. The danger lies in falling under the spell of a specific picture and claiming a privileged position for it. Since it would not only deny the limitations of the specific angle, but also prevent further explorations, this spell must be broken by relentlessly showing the contradictions that result from fixing the boundaries from one perspective. Pointing out the contradictions that follow from such a closure is an activity that Derrida calls 'deconstruction'.

The discussion so far has actually been a deconstruction of the concepts of representation without slipping into the post-structural discourse. One motivation for taking this approach was the desire to show that post-structuralism is not only a form of discourse analysis, but that it constitutes a theoretical stance that has practical implications for science and technology. Another motivation was the need to resist the lure of the deconstructive discourse as long as possible – to avoid slipping into it too easily – since there is always the risk, often underestimated by philosophers, of trying to play the game without knowing the field. However, since the notion of representation is philosophically important, the ramifications of distributed representation should be made explicit.

Distributed semiotics

Any theory of representation flows from a specific theory of the nature of the sign. In most semiotic systems the sign acquires meaning by virtue of referring to something – it represents the referent. Saussure (1974) presented us with a system of *distributed* semiotics by arguing that the meaning of a sign is a consequence of its relationships to all the other signs in the system. Meaning is therefore not a specific characteristic of any discrete unit, but the result of a system of differences. In order to generate the meaning of a sign, not only *that* sign, but the whole system, is involved – the meaning is distributed. However, since he maintains the distinction between signifier and signified, his system remains representational. Although he implements the system in a distributed way, he does not want to relinquish the upper level of the Tower Bridge picture. It is exactly this point that Derrida targets in his assault on Saussurian semiotics.

In a system of distributed semiotics the sign is constituted by the sum of its relationships to other signs. Derrida calls the relationship between any two signs, a 'trace'. The trace itself, though, has no meaning, no ideational content that can be made explicit. It operates at the level of the sign itself, not at a meta-level above or below the sign. Understood in this way, a trace is equivalent to a weight in a neural network. The significance of a node in a network is not a result of some characteristic of the node itself; it is a result of the pattern of weighted inputs and outputs that connects the node to other nodes. The weight, just like the trace, does not stand for anything specific.

In supplanting a general theory of semiotics with a 'science' of grammatology,

Derrida explicitly denies a theory of representation. He deconstructs the Tower, leaving us only the material bottom level. The system is no longer governed from a metaphysical exterior, nor from an internal centre of command. It is constituted only by the distributed interaction of traces in a network (Derrida 1982: 3–27). Furthermore, Derrida's notion of *différance*, as presented in the citation referred to here, manifests itself in connectionist models, specifically in recurrent neural networks. This type of network has many feedback loops: the output of a certain node can become the input to the same node, with or without passing through other nodes in the process. The activity of a node is therefore not only determined by its differences from other nodes, but also deferred until its own activity (and those of others) has been reflected back upon it. In this complex pattern of interaction it is impossible to say that a certain sign (or node) represents anything specific. A strong theory of representation will always presuppose the metaphysics of presence. It actually argues for two systems – the signs themselves and, external to them, the meaning of the signs – which are made present to each other through the process of representation. A distributed theory of semiotics problematises this division. It again argues that there is nothing outside the system of signs which could determine the trace, since the 'outside' itself does not escape the logic of the trace. Should you attempt to find the origin of the trace outside, you would be confronted with the same fragmentations, movements and erasures. Inside and outside refer to each other in a 'generalised reference'; we have here a distributed representation confined to the level of the signifier. Derrida (1982: 24) formulates it as follows:

> Since the trace is not a presence but the simulacrum of a presence that dislocates itself, displaces itself, refers itself, it properly has no site – erasure belongs to its structure. . . . The paradox of such a structure, in the language of metaphysics, is an inversion of metaphysical concepts, which produces the following effect: the present becomes the sign of the sign, the trace of the trace. It is no longer what every reference refers to in the last analysis. It becomes a function in a structure of generalized reference. It is a trace, and a trace of the erasure of the trace.

The ease with which we fall for a general theory of representation can perhaps be explained by the importance of the *image* in our culture. 'We give preference to sensing "through the eyes" not only for taking action, but even when we have no praxis in view' (Derrida 1983: 4). When we say that an image speaks a thousand words – meaning that an image is somehow more powerful than language – we fall prey to the metaphysics of presence. We believe that an image bears its meaning on its face, that it escapes the play of referral described by a distributed semiotics. A text may have to be interpreted, but an image speaks *directly*, or so we believe. This notion is strongly resisted by post-structural theory. An argument against representation is at the same time an argument for the textual nature of the image itself (Derrida 1976: 36).

When we deny the possibility of a theory of representation, the question concerning the relationship between the distributed system and the world does not, however, disappear. An answer can be attempted from a connectionist perspective. In a representational system, the representation and that which is being represented operate at different logical levels; they belong to different categories. This is not the case with a neural network. There is no difference in kind between the sensory traces entering the network and the traces that interact inside the network. In a certain sense we have the outside *repeated,* or *reiterated*, on the inside, thereby deconstructing the distinction between outside and inside. The gap between the two has collapsed.[11]

The theory of representation, combined with our love of the image, is ultimately narcissistic. This narcissism is consummated in our attempt to simulate human intelligence on a computer, through the use of abstract rationality and a strong theory of representation.

The notion of the machine

We often think of machines as if they contain something dehumanising. At best, they are seen as useful, even essential, tools; at worst, as destroyers of the soul. It is this double relationship – dependence and abhorrence – that lends such a strange flavour to the attempts to copy living intelligence on a dead machine. For many this is the ultimate quest of modern science, the last grail. For others it becomes the prime symbol of an instrumental understanding of human beings, an approach that supposedly denies important human values. In one sense these two sentiments are not so far apart: the first group claims that what is essentially human can be represented in a machine; the second group fears that when that happens there will be nothing left to claim as the mark of being human. Both are mesmerised by the idea of being reduced to a machine.

But what exactly is this thing called 'human' we want to simulate on a machine? What is the original we desire a simulacrum for? If we wish to represent a human, we must believe that we already possess a theory of what it is to be human. Some of the colours of such a theory (in a representational guise) are shown in the selection of the first attributes of the simulacrum – an abstract, androgynous intelligence, explicitly called 'artificial'. The project remains one of representing inside the simulacrum something the true form of which can be found only outside it. But the 'logic' of the trace disturbs both the representation (inside) and the to-be-represented (outside). When the closure of the inside is breached, we discover a different mimesis, one that is constituted by a reflexive process of mutual definition (see Clark 1985). The inside and the outside become intertwined. Once we let go of our nostalgia for something really real, something that can be faithfully copied, we move into what Baudrillard (1984) calls the 'hyperreal'. When we say that the inside and the outside are folded into each other, it has implications not only for our understanding of the dynamics of a complex system, but also, as argued above, for our understanding of reality. Since 'reality' is primarily made accessible in linguistic terms, our understanding of the world is subjected to the logic of the trace. The world is no longer a simple origin of meaning. This state of affairs is intensified by the way in which our understanding of the world is increasingly mediated by technology (computers) and the media (especially television). We are confronted no longer by reality, but by a simulacrum of reality, a hyperreality. These notions have been analysed, with specific reference to postmodern American culture, by both Baudrillard and Umberto Eco (1987).

Baudrillard (1984: 254) explains the move into the hyperreal as an effect of the 'liquidation of all referentials'. Our systems of signs are no longer anchored in the real world; they float on our screens and multiply in our computers and databases. There is no longer a 'real' and an 'imaginary' (the interpreted meaning of the real); everything has collapsed into the level of signs and their interactions – a 'precession of simulacra'. This is how he formulates it:

> It is no longer a question of imitation, nor of reduplication, nor even of paradox. It is rather a question of substituting signs of the real for the real itself, that is, an operation to deter every real process by its operational double, a metastable, programmatic, perfect descriptive machine which provides all the signs of the real and shortcircuits all its vicissitudes. . . . A hyperreal henceforth sheltered from the imaginary, and from any distinction between the real and the imaginary, leaving room only for the orbital recurrence of models and the simulated generation of difference.
>
> (254)

As replacement for the concept of representation, Baudrillard chooses the notion of 'simulation'. A simulation does not attempt to represent some essential abstraction of something real; it rather attempts to *repeat* it, thereby undermining the distinction between the real and the simulated.

Whereas representation tries to absorb simulation by interpreting it as false representation, simulation envelops the whole edifice of representation as itself a simulacrum. These would be the successive phases of the image:

- it is the reflection of a basic reality
- it masks and perverts a basic reality
- it masks the *absence* of a basic reality
- it bears no relation to any reality whatever: it is its own pure simulacrum.

(256)

Let me illustrate this with a practical example. Neural networks are normally 'simulated' on a digital computer. The computer itself does not contain a network of interconnected nodes, but it can be made to behave as if it does. Now connect a microphone to the computer by means of which the 'network' can be provided with information, and use the output of the computer to produce some effect, like switching on a motor. This system can perform a task (e.g. open a gate when a car approaches) that is associated with the special capabilities of a neural network (distinguishing the sound of a car from other noises). It is now possible to ask whether we are working with a simulation or not. The point is, however, that the answer does not really matter. Since the system behaves as if a network is doing the work, the distinction between a 'real' network and a 'simulated' one evaporates.

These thoughts have important consequences for the issues now under consideration – the distinction between human and machine and the quest for machine intelligence. The quest may be failing as a result of the theory of representation. This theory makes the metaphysical assumption that something essentially human has to be represented in an abstract way, instead of realising that, following the logic of the simulacrum, we have one machine that has to repeat or reiterate another reflexively. The question shifts from 'How do we simulate a human on a machine?' to 'What kind of a machine is this thing sometimes called human?'

This is the question that bothered Freud throughout his career, from the early *Project* (1895, published posthumously in 1950) to the famous 'Note on the "Mystic Writing-Pad" ' (1925). He tried to conceive of the psyche in terms of the metaphors of traces and machines (Bass 1984: 77), without resorting to the use of an abstract notion of cognition. The network model of the *Project*, and the simple machine known as the Mystic Writing-Pad, finally combine a certain understanding of 'machine' with a certain understanding of 'writing'. For Freud, however, the Mystic Writing-Pad remains a metaphor; it 'represents' the working of the psyche. In his reading of Freud, Derrida (1978: 199) urges us not only to use the metaphor, but to move beyond it:

> Psychical *content* will be *represented* by a text whose essence is irreducibly graphic. The *structure* of the psychical *apparatus* will be *represented* by a writing machine. What questions will these representations impose upon us? We shall not have to ask if a writing apparatus – for example, the one described in the 'Note on the Mystic Writing-Pad' – is a *good* metaphor for representing the working of the psyche, but rather what apparatus we must create in order to represent psychical writing; and we shall have to ask what the imitation, projected and liberated in a machine, of something like psychical writing might mean. And not if the psyche is indeed a kind of text, but: what is a text, and what must the psyche be if it can be represented by a text? For if there is neither machine nor text without psychical origin, there is no domain of the psychic without text. Finally, what must be the relationship between psyche, writing, and spacing for

such a metaphoric transition to be possible, not only, nor primarily, within theoretical discourse, but within the history of psyche, text, and technology?

Derrida points here to Freud's stopping short of 'any examination of *representation itself* or the implications of the "resemblance" between psyche and machine' (Clark 1985: 310). This prevents him from realising that the psyche is just a 'writing machine', nothing more and nothing less. The notion of machine is important to Derrida (Bass 1984: 77). After the removal of the metaphysical dimension of both language and the brain, we are left with the comparative leanness of the material machine.[12] The machine is complex not only in the sense of having a complicated structure and parts, but also in the sense of undergoing endless repetitions, transformations and interactions in a way that is truly distributed.

It bears repetition that an argument against representation is not anti-scientific at all. It is merely an argument against a particular scientific strategy that assumes complexity can be reduced to specific features and then represented in a machine. Instead, it is an argument for the appreciation of the nature of complexity, something that can perhaps be 'repeated' in a machine, should the machine itself be complex enough to cope with the distributed nature of complexity.

Whether our technology can manufacture such a machine remains an open question. What is clear, however, is that the computer will continue to play a paradoxical role in these developments. On the one hand, it has been the perfect vehicle for attempts to implement the metaphysics of representation. On the other hand, it may yet become the distributed writing machine that runs by itself 'as if on wheels'.

Let me reiterate the above argument as it is central to this book. Models based on formal symbol systems have the classical theory of representation built in. The main problem with representation lies in the relationship between the symbols and their meaning. There are two ways of establishing this relationship. One can either claim that the relationship is 'natural', determined in some *a priori* fashion, or one has to settle for an external designer determining this relationship. The first option is a strongly metaphysical one since it claims that meaning is determined by some kind of fundamental, all-embracing law. Such an approach has to be excluded here because the main thrust of my argument is that an understanding of complexity should be developed without recourse to metaphysical cornerstones. The second option – where the relationships are the result of the decisions made by a designer – is acceptable as long as an active, external agent can be assumed to be present. When a well-framed system is being modelled on a computer by a well-informed modeller, this could well be the case. However, when we deal with autonomous, self-organising systems with a high degree of complexity, the second option becomes metaphysical as well. As soon as we drop the notion of representation, these metaphysical problems disappear.

We can still have a machine capable of encoding information from its environment and acting on the basis of it, without having to cluster its internal mechanisms into representational blobs. That does not imply that the internal structure of such a non-representational, distributed system will be one continuous, homogeneous whole. It could well be differentiated into several functional sub-structures, but they will then be *functional* units, not *representational* units. Most of these units will probably have a distributed structure and will have a high level of interconnection with other units. The development of internal structure will be analysed in detail when we turn to the process of self-organisation in the next chapter. At this point we should just add that there is no guarantee that connectionist models will eventually simulate the brain or natural language completely. However, with the rejection of metaphysical cornerstones, the problem becomes a contingent one that cannot be given an *a priori* answer.

The effects of representation on the relationship between science and theory

Before turning to self-organisation I will briefly discuss some consequences of a distributed theory for the status of scientific theories. One of the central values of science is that of objectivity. The principle of objective reason can only function if it is assumed that the scientist can see things as they really are. The search for objectivity, however, inevitably introduces a rift between the scientist as knowing subject, on the one hand, and the object of study, as represented in some purified form, on the other hand. In an essay on the role and status of the university, Derrida (1983) analyses this issue in some detail:

> The modern dominance of the principle of reason had to go hand in hand with the interpretation of the essence of beings as objects, an object present as representation (*Vorstellung*), an object placed and positioned before a subject. This latter, a man who says 'I', an ego certain of itself, thus ensures his own technical mastery over the totality of what is. The 're-' of *repraesentatio* also expresses the movement that accounts for – 'renders reason to' – a thing whose presence is encountered by rendering it present, by bringing it to the subject of representation, to the knowing self. ... But it is true that a caricature of representational man, in the Heideggerian sense, would readily endow him with hard eyes permanently open to a nature that he is to dominate, to rape if necessary, by fixing it in front of himself, or by swooping down on it like a bird of prey.
> (9–10)

Relinquishing a theory of representation thus implies a deconstruction of rigid borders between science and theory. If true objectivity is no longer possible, theory spills over into all levels of scientific activity. This loss of clear distinctions between theory and praxis has ramifications not only for science, but also for theory. Theory can no longer be practised for its own sake, as a search for pure knowledge.

Derrida claims that it was possible, somewhere in the past, to believe in 'pure' science, unencumbered by pressures from the state and unhindered by financial constraints. This is no longer possible, or, more accurately, actually never was.

> Within each of these fields [theoretical physics, astrophysics, chemistry, molecular biology, and so forth] – and they are more interrelated than ever – the so-called basic philosophical questions no longer simply take the form of abstract, sometimes epistemological questions raised after the fact: they arise at the very heart of scientific research in the widest variety of ways. One can no longer distinguish between technology on the one hand and theory, science and rationality on the other.
>
> (12)

At the same time that science loses the clarity of this objectivity, philosophy loses the luxury of avoiding the contingent. This will be a lasting characteristic of postmodernity, namely that scientists and philosophers alike have lost their innocence. Since a certain theory of representation implies a certain theory of meaning – and meaning is what we live by – our choice of such a theory has important ethical implications. I will return to these issues in the final chapter.

6 Self-organisation in complex systems

So far a lot of attention has been paid to the characteristics of the structure of complex systems. In this chapter the focus will be on how that structure comes about, develops and changes. The notion of 'structure' pertains to the internal mechanism developed by the system to receive, encode, transform and store information on the one hand, and to react to such information by some form of output on the other. The main burden of the argument will be to show that internal structure can evolve without the intervention of an external designer or the presence of some centralised form of internal control. If the capacities of the system satisfy a number of constraints, it can develop a distributed form of internal structure through a process of self-organisation. This process is such that structure is neither a passive reflection of the outside, nor a result of active, pre-programmed internal factors, but the result of a complex interaction between the environment, the present state of the system and the history of the system.

Most philosophical positions throughout the Western intellectual tradition have been sceptical about the *spontaneous* emergence of order and structure. In the absence of a rational explanation for such emergence, some kind of organising agent – God (as the ultimate designer) or some other *a priori* principle – was usually postulated. Yet self-organisation is neither a mystic process nor a random one, and should not be in conflict with any of our normal sensibilities. That is what I hope to show in this chapter.

Several examples of self-organising systems will be discussed later, but here a simple (and very limited) example will help to introduce the basic ideas of self-organisation. Consider a school of fish in a dam, and assume we can measure their general well-being by looking at the size of the school. The condition of the fish would depend on a large number of factors, including the availability of food, the temperature of the water, the amount of available oxygen and light, the time of year, etc. As these conditions vary, the size of the school of fish will adjust itself optimally to suit prevailing conditions, despite the fact that each individual fish can only look after its own interests. The system of the school as a whole organises itself to ensure the best match between the system and its environment. This organisation is also adaptive in the sense that the school will be sensitive to changing conditions in the light of past experience. There is no agent that decides for the school what should happen, nor does each individual fish understand the complexity of the situation. The organisation of the school emerges as a result of the interaction between the various constituents of the system and its environment.

A last introductory remark is perhaps necessary. The basic characteristics and principles of self-organisation described below are fairly general, and will of course overlap with the general characteristics of complex systems discussed in Chapter 1. They have been abstracted from a number of examples quite diverse in nature, therefore the full set of characteristics will not necessarily be present in each of them. However, the more complex the system is, the more of these characteristics will be apparent. The aim remains to provide an understanding of the dynamics of self-organisation as a *general* property of complex systems.

KEY ASPECTS

Towards a definition of self-organisation

Given the difficulty in defining complex phenomena, a working definition of self-organisation will be provided, illuminated by a number of characteristics and examples:

> *The capacity for self-organisation is a property of complex systems which enables them to develop or change internal structure spontaneously and adaptively in order to cope with, or manipulate, their environment.*

The kind of system we are interested in is best exemplified by the brain. Within certain given constraints – including physical, biological and genetic ones – the brain has to develop an understanding of its environment, and be able to operate effectively in that environment. Since it is implausible that the brain contains, *ab initio*, a programme that can cope with all eventualities, we can safely assume that the brain has to have the ability to *learn*. The necessary changes in structure that enable the brain to *remember* what has been learnt must therefore come about spontaneously.

Different systems that share the property of self-organisation will not necessarily exhibit the same range of characteristics. A living cell can certainly be classified as self-organising, but its internal structure will be more stable than that of, say, the economic system of a country. An economic system is self-organising in the sense that it changes its internal structure in response to a large number of factors (money supply, growth rate, political stability, natural disasters, etc.). Although the interaction of all these factors is too complex to allow the construction of a deterministic model, large-scale intervention in the internal structure of the system is possible (revaluation of the currency, adjustment of interest rates, etc.). The effects of these interventions, however, are only predictable in the short term since the spontaneous adjustment of the system involves the complex inter-action of too many factors – many of which cannot be controlled at all.

Another example of a self-organising system is that of language. In order to enable communication, language must have a recognisable structure. To be able to maintain its function in vastly different circumstances, the struc-ture must be able to adjust – especially as far as *meaning* is concerned. Because many individuals are involved in using the same language, these adjustments cannot merely take place at the level of individual decisions. Change results from the *interaction* of large numbers of individuals.[1] Systems of social interaction, i.e. cultural systems, share many of the char-acteristics of linguistic systems. The models of complex systems developed here have certain implications for theory of language, as well as for a number of more general philosophical and ethical issues. These will be discussed in the final chapter.

These examples show that self-organisation can work at different levels and according to varying constraints. Despite differences between various instances of complex systems, however, the process of self-organisation has a number of general characteristics, to which we shall now turn.

ATTRIBUTES OF SELF-ORGANISING SYSTEMS

Despite important differences between various self-organising, complex systems with different functions, there are shared attributes that conform to the framework of the general model for complex systems. As we argued in Chapter 1, a complex system is constituted by a large number of simple units forming nodes in a network with a high level of non-linear intercon-nection. The behaviour of a system is not determined primarily by the properties of individual components of the system, but is the result of complex patterns of interaction. General attributes of self-organising systems include the following:

(i)   The structure of the system is not the result of an *a priori* design, nor is it determined directly by external conditions. It is a result of *interaction* between the system and its environment.

(ii)   The internal structure of the system can adapt dynamically to changes in the environment, even if these changes are not regular.

(iii) Self-organisation is not merely the result of processes like feedback or regulation that can be described linearly. It involves higher-order, non-linear processes that cannot be modelled by sets of linear differential equations. A thermostat that responds to its environ-ment by switching on and off is *not* an example of self-organisation.

(iv)   Self-organisation is an emergent property of a system as a whole (or of large enough sub-systems). The system's individual components only operate on *local* information and general principles. The macroscopic behaviour emerges from microscopic interactions that by themselves have a very meagre information content (only traces). By confining your analysis to the microscopic level, it becomes possible to explain the behaviour of each element in terms of a number of simple transformations. Simple, local interactions can result in complex behaviour when viewed macroscopically.

(v) Self-organising systems *increase* in complexity. Since they have to 'learn' from experience, they have to 'remember' previously encountered situations and compare them with new ones. If more 'previous information' can be stored, the system will be able to make better comparisons. This increase in complexity implies a local reversal of entropy, which necessitates a flow of energy or information through the systems. The increase in complexity may also form part of the explanation why self-organising systems tend to age. Since these systems are bound by the finite constraints of the physical world, they inevitably become saturated at some point.

(vi) Self-organisation is impossible without some form of memory, a point closely related to the previous one. Without memory, the system can do no better than merely mirror the environment. A self-organising system therefore always has a *history*. This diachronic component cannot be ignored in any description of the system since previous conditions of the system form vital influences on present behaviour. Memory, on the other hand, is impossible without some form of selective forgetting. Just piling up information without some form of integration renders it insignificant. Integration is not 'performed' through some form of decision-making within the system. Information that is not used simply fades away. This process not only creates space in memory, but, more importantly, it provides a measure of the significance of the stored pattern. The more something is used, the stronger its 'representation' in memory will be. Use it or lose it. Self-organisation is only possible if the system can remember *and* forget.

(vii) Since the self-organising process is not guided or determined by specific goals, it is often difficult to talk about the *function* of such a system. As soon as we introduce the notion of function, we run the risk either of anthropomorphising, or of introducing an external reason for the structure of the system, exactly those aspects we are trying to avoid. When a system is described within the context of a larger system, it is possible to talk of a function of the sub-system *only within that context*. We can talk about the 'function' of the endocrine system of a lion with reference to the lion, but then it is difficult to simultaneously talk about the function of the lion itself. We can talk about the 'function' of predators in an ecosystem, but then not of the function of the ecosystem. The notion of function is intimately linked to our *descriptions* of complex systems. The process of self-organisation cannot be driven by the attempt to perform a function; it is rather the result of an evolutive process whereby a system will simply not survive if it cannot adapt to more complex circumstances.

(viii) Similarly, it is not possible to give crudely reductionistic descriptions of self-organising systems. Since microscopic units do not 'know' about large-scale effects, while at the same time these effects manifest themselves in collections that do not involve anything besides these microscopic units, the various 'levels' of the system cannot be given independent descriptions. The levels are in principle intertwined. The resistance to using a reductionist discourse when describing emergent properties does not, however, imply any resistance to materialist principles.

In a nutshell, the process of self-organisation in complex systems works in the following way. Clusters of information from the external world flow into the system. This information will influence the interaction of some of the components in the system – it will alter the values of the weights in the network. Following Hebb's rule (discussed in Chapter 1), if a certain cluster is present regularly, the system will acquire a stable set of weights that 'represents' that cluster, i.e. a certain pattern of activity will be caused in the system each time that specific cluster is present. If two clusters are regularly present together, the system will automatically develop an association between the two. For example, if a certain state of affairs regularly causes harm to the system, the system will associate that condition with harm *without having to know beforehand that the condition is harmful.* As the system encounters different conditions in the environment, it will generate new structures to 'represent' those conditions, within the constraints determined by the amount of memory available to the system. This process can be described mathematically (Grossberg 1987, 1988; Kauffman 1993; Kohonen 1988), but it does not differ in principle from Freud's neurological model of how the brain develops its structure (Freud 1950).

What remains to be discussed now are the actual principles by which the interactions within a system are adjusted.

Basic principles of self-organisation

Self-organisation can be modelled in more than one way, but most models rest on a system of simple processing units that are interconnected in a network. I will stick to the neural network model.[2] To repeat briefly, a neural network consists of a number of simple neurons, interconnected by synapses. These synapses have different strengths, which means that the neurons interact with each other in a complex, non-linear way. The system is best visualised as a network of interconnected nodes where each interconnection has a certain strength or 'weight'. Since the nodes are all basically similar, the behaviour of the network is determined by the values of the weights, values which can be adjusted. Adjustments are determined by simple rules based only on information available locally at the nodes involved. One such rule would be to increase the value of a weight if both neurons interconnected by it are active (Hebb's rule). In such a way, the network can develop patterns of activity based on the dynamic structure of the interconnections.

But how can the structure of a system also develop in response to conditions in the environment around it? This is only possible if information can enter the system from outside. At least some interconnections therefore have to terminate in sensors or transducers that can sense aspects of the environment and stimulate the system accordingly.[3] Some event in the environment will now cause some activity inside the system, and this activity can be used to alter the structure of the system, again only by means of information available locally at each node – a global perspective is not necessary. On condition that the information is not fed into a homogeneous network in a symmetrical way, the nodes of the network will be activated irregularly. Certain groups of neurons will be more active than others. By simply increasing the weights associated with active nodes, and decreasing the rest, this pattern of activity will be reinforced. If the external event does not occur again, this pattern will eventually fade away (be forgotten) or be eroded by other patterns. If the event is significant, in the sense that it occurs often, the pattern will be reinforced each time the event occurs. In this way the system develops a stable structure that enables it to recognise important events through a process of self-organisation.

Since the most important aspect of self-organisation is the emergence of structure through the activity of microscopic units that do not have access to global patterns, the principles that determine the behaviours of weights and nodes locally are very important. The following list provides a number of preconditions for self-organisation in any system and they are fundamental to the understanding thereof:[4]

(i)   The system consists of a *large number* of microscopic elements or units that are relatively undifferentiated initially, i.e. there is no need for predefined structure.[5] In neural network terms this means that the network starts off with random values for all the weights.

(ii) The strengths of interconnections change as a result of *local information* only. These changes are often self-maintaining (positive feedback is involved), and cause the system to move away from the undifferentiated state.

(iii) There is *competition* among the units. Competing for limited resources is the basic driving force behind the development of structure. Stronger units thrive at the expense of others. If resources were limitless, i.e. if growth could take place unrestricted, no meaningful structure would evolve. Boundaries, limits and constraints are preconditions for structure.

(iv)   There is also *co-operation* among at least some units. If only single units won, the resulting structure would be too simple for self-organisation to evolve. Co-operation is also necessary to form associations among patterns. Mutual reinforcement and co-operation are preconditions for a rich, meaningful structure.

(v)   The interactions among units have to be *non-linear*. Small changes must be able to cause large effects, and the combination of patterns should result in the formation of new ones, not merely in linear combinations of the constituents.

(vi)   An important secondary principle is *symmetry-breaking*. If the initial state of the system is fully homogeneous, the evolving structure could be too symmetrical. This will inhibit the development of complex structure. Symmetry-breaking is usually achieved spontaneously by means of missing or incorrect connections (or other happenings of chance), as well as by the non-linearity of the system and the resulting sensitivity to small fluctuations.

(vii) Another secondary principle is that of *entrainment*. Some patterns will catch others in their wake in the sense that they will start appearing in concert.[6] This process increases the order in a system and facilitates the formation of associations through resonance.

(viii) A last, and a most important, principle requires that the *memory* of the system be stored in a *distributed fashion*. The importance of memory has already been stated, and in neural networks the connection strengths, or weights, perform the function of storing information. Specific weights cannot stand for specific bits of symbolic information since this would imply that the information should be interpretable at the level of that weight. Since each weight only has access to local levels of activity, it cannot perform the more complex function of standing for a concept. Complex concepts would involve a pattern of activity over several units. Weights store information at a sub-symbolic level, as *traces* of memory. The fact that information is distributed over many units not only increases the robustness of the system, but makes the association of different patterns an inherent characteristic of the system – they overlap in principle. (The notion of distributedness received detailed attention in Chapter 5.)

The way in which these basic principles enable the process of self-organisation will be elucidated as we continue, especially when we discuss the 'selection' theories of brain development. In the following section an argument will be presented that claims not only that complex systems will organise their structure, but that they will tend to do so in an optimal way.

SELF-ORGANISED CRITICALITY

When we are faced with unexpected occurrences, especially when they have catastrophic results, we tend to ascribe their cause to a rare combination of unlikely circumstances. When we have to explain the crash of the stock-market, an earthquake, or the sudden outbreak of political violence, we try to find a number of factors that combined to cause it, often with the hope of showing that the chances of the same combination of factors occurring again are slim. This kind of analysis, however, is the result of trying to explain the behaviour of large, complex systems by extrapolating from the behaviour of small, simple systems. Unfortunately this extrapolation fails. Complex systems – in which many factors interact in an asynchronous way – display unexpected, often unpredictable behaviour. Any analysis that ignores the possibility of self-organising behaviour by a complex system will be seriously lacking in explanatory power.

A very useful concept in the analysis of complex systems, introduced by Per Bak, Kan Chen and colleagues (Bak and Chen 1991), is that of self-organised criticality. This concept helps us to understand some of the global features of systems consisting of large amounts of elements that interact locally.

> . . . many composite systems naturally evolve to a critical state in which a minor event starts a chain reaction that can affect any number of elements in the system. Although composite systems produce more minor events than catastrophes, chain reactions of all sizes are an integral part of the dynamics. According to the theory, the mechanism that leads to minor events is the same one that leads to major events. Furthermore, composite systems never reach equilibrium but instead evolve from one meta-stable state to the next.
>
> Self-organized criticality is a holistic theory: the global features, such as the relative number of large and small events, do not depend on the microscopic mechanisms. Consequently, global features of the system cannot be understood by analyzing the parts separately. To our knowledge, self-organized criticality is the only model or mathematical description that has led to a holistic theory for dynamic systems.
>
> (Bak and Chen 1991: 26)

A simple illustration will clarify the principles involved. If you pour grains of sand onto a small disc, a pyramid of sand will form. The height of the pyramid will depend mainly on the size of the disc and the characteristics of the sand. Once the average height is more or less attained, the sand will start to roll down. But *how* does it roll down? Consider a small heap that has reached its 'critical' height and add more sand grain by grain. These grains do not fall off one by one. They may stick to the pile, or cause little avalanches. Two aspects of this simple model are important. In the first place, the heap will maintain itself around its critical height. When it becomes too low, more grains will stick; when it is high, more will fall off. In the second place, any individual grain of sand may cause an avalanche of any size: sometimes just a few grains, sometimes a landslide. The changes will not always be the same, depending on whether the heap is above or below the critical point, but the effect of any single grain is never predictable. The vital point to note here is the following: the system organises itself towards the critical point where single events have the widest possible range of effects. Put differently, the system tunes itself towards optimum sensitivity to external inputs.

A method often employed to visualise the behaviour of a system is to describe it in state-space. State-space has a separate dimension for each independent variable of the system. In the case of three variables, say temperature, volume and pressure, the state-space will be three-dimensional. In the case of a thousand variables, as one would have in a network with a thousand nodes, the state-space will be thousand-dimensional. Every possible state of the system will then be characterised by a unique point in state-space, and the dynamics of the system will form trajectories through state-space. When a number of trajectories lead towards a point (or area) in state-space, that point (or area) is an 'attractor', and represents a stable state of the system. When trajectories all lead away from a point, that point is unstable – a 'repellor'. A point that has trajectories leading towards it as well as away from it is known as 'meta-stable'.[7]

A network of nodes has many degrees of freedom, and therefore a large state-space. It is difficult or impossible to *visualise* such a state-space, but the concept remains useful. In a very stable system there will be one, or only a few strong attractors. The system will quickly come to rest in one of these, and will not move to another one easily. The resulting behaviour of the system is not very interesting. On the other hand, in a very unstable system, there will be no strong attractors, and the system will just jump around chaotically. The theory of self-organised criticality tells us the following. A self-organising system will try to balance itself at a critical point between rigid order and chaos. It will try to optimise the number of attractors without becoming unstable. Why is this important? It is clear that a system that only behaves chaotically is useless. On the other hand, a system that is too stable is also handicapped. If each required state of the system has to be represented by a strong, stable attractor, a lot of the resources of the system will be tied up (limiting all the degrees of freedom at a certain point means that many nodes must participate), and the capacity of the system for adaptation will be badly impaired. Furthermore, movement from one stable state to another will require very strong perturbations. For this reason the system will respond sluggishly to changes in the environment. However, with the system poised at the point of criticality, the number of stable states will not only be optimised, but the system will also be able to change its state with the least amount of effort.

It should be clear that the principle of competition is the driving force behind this behaviour. Each node in the network will tend to dominate as large a portion of state-space as possible, and nodes therefore compete for the available resources. Inputs to the system that do not have much variety will be represented by a few strong attractors. As the inputs increase in variability, the system will tend towards the critical point where it is optimised for flexibility. If the information that the system has to cope with becomes more than the inherent capability of the system, the system will be forced beyond the critical point. It will not be able to produce any stable attractors and chaos will ensue. For this reason, the resources of a self-organising system should be neither over-extended, nor under-extended.

Another aspect of self-organisation that is illuminated by these phenomena is the emergence of large-scale features when there are only local interactions among units. In this regard, some interesting arguments are put forward by Kauffman (1991). He demonstrates – in simple networks where each node is either on or off, and can only have two inputs – the formation of order through 'cores' of stability that form in the network. This stability then 'percolates' through the network as adjacent nodes are drawn into stability by the already stable group. The result is that the network is 'partitioned into an unchanging frozen core and islands of changing elements' (67). Fluctuating groups are thus isolated, and order is imposed upon the network. The model can be made more complex networks by imposing certain 'biases' on the nodes. These will suppress signals below a certain threshold – another example of non-linear interaction. The size of the bias has an important effect: if it is too high, the network will be too stable, if it is too low, the network will be chaotic. The bias therefore provides a mechanism through which the system can adjust itself to remain at the critical level even when the complexity of the external world fluctuates.

The tendency a system has to move towards criticality results in an increase in complexity. What researchers like Kauffman and Bak are trying to show is that this tendency is an intrinsic characteristic of complex systems. Once a system has the capacity to self-organise, there is a 'natural' drive to optimise the organisation. The drive towards a more complex structure is a result of 'economic' reasons: resources cannot be wasted. In this respect there is an observation to be made. The critical state of a system is often referred to as being 'on the edge of chaos' (Lewin 1993). The word 'chaos' is then used in the technical sense (deterministic chaos, the object of study of 'chaos theory'), and the argument is made that critical organisation is the result of some 'deep' principle uncovered by chaos theory. To argue that self-organised criticality can be explained through 'economic' principles, without relying on any arguments from chaos theory, is both a weaker and more general claim. This does not necessarily imply that chaos theory is mistaken. The claim is merely made to reinforce the argument (made in the Preface) that 'complexity' is a much more general category than 'chaos'. This will be emphasised in the next section when we explore some of the evolutionary aspects of self-organisation.

ORGANISATION THROUGH SELECTION

Preceding sections focused mainly on the internal structure of complex systems. Self-organisation was described in terms of general principles, with a focus on the necessary internal relationships among the components of the system that allow interesting dynamic behaviour. In this section I will examine the application of the principle of selection – a notion borrowed from the theory of evolution – to the development of structure in complex systems. Once again, the brain will serve as a central example.

Complex systems are open systems – systems that interact with their environment, not only in terms of energy, but also in terms of information. These systems must be able to adapt to changes in the environment, and therefore their internal structure must be influenced in some way by external conditions. Often the very distinction between 'inside' and 'outside' the system becomes problematic.

Which are the possible coping mechanisms open to a system faced with changing external conditions? Two extreme positions can be identified. At the one extreme, the structure of the system is fully defined *a priori*. This would mean that the system is 'hard-wired', and that all possible eventualities will have to be catered for in the fixed, internal structure of the system. Apart from the loss in adaptivity, such systems may become too cumbersome in complex situations. Under less complex conditions, 'hard-wired' systems, operating on simple control principles, may be an adequate solution, but this is not a plausible option for the kind of complex systems we are interested in. At the other extreme we may have systems with no independent internal structure at all, but where the structure is fully determined by the conditions in the environment. A system which merely mimics the environment directly will not be capable of acting in that environment since it will be fully at its mercy. To be able to interpret its environment, the system must have at least the following two attributes: some form of resistance to change, and some mechanism for comparing different conditions in order to determine whether there has been enough change to warrant some response. Both these attributes merely translate into the need for a form of memory – without resistance to change, memory is impossible. If the self-organising capabilities of such a system are adequate, it will then *learn* to cope with a changing environment.

We are of course not limited to the two extremes. When considering a biological system, we encounter a number of constraints. Living systems have to operate in extremely complex conditions, and therefore adaptivity is of prime importance. To complicate matters, they are also subjected to certain temporal constraints. The survival of an organism depends on responding appropriately, and in time. Under certain critical conditions there may not be enough time or margin for error to allow an adaptive response, and predetermined 'hard-wired' reactions may be the only solution (e.g. a new-born mammal cannot afford to first 'learn' how to use its intestines). This indicates a need for some form of balance between the two extremes. But where does this balance lie? How much is genetically encoded and how much can be ascribed to responses to the environment? In the context of the brain, what we have here is a reformulation of the nature/nurture dilemma.

Fortunately, the need to indicate precisely where the balance lies becomes less pressing if we can show that the same mechanisms implement both the predetermined and adaptive needs of the system.

Learning through selection

The theory of evolution attempts to explain how biological systems, from generation to generation, develop certain capabilities that enhance their survivability. This theory largely explains the predetermined side of biological systems' behaviour, and does not really say anything about the adaptive behaviour of any specific organism. To ensure its survival, an organism must not only learn to cope with its changing environment, but it must do so within its own lifetime, in what is known as 'somatic time'. If we can link the notion of self-organisation to that of evolution, i.e. if we can develop a more general understanding of the notion of selection, it would be possible to argue that the distinction between predetermined and adaptive behaviour is not rigid.[8] To an extent, this synthesis has been attempted by two neurobiologists, Jean-Pierre Changeaux and Gerald Edelman. They have, in slightly different ways, extended the notion of evolutionary selection to include the adaptive behaviour found in networks of neurons. Edelman (1987) calls it 'Neural Darwinism'.

How can a system respond to its environment? Changeaux *et al.* (1984) mention two mechanisms similar to those referred to above:

- An instructive mechanism where the environment *imposes* order directly on the structure of the system.
- A selective (Darwinian) mechanism where the increase in order is a result of an interaction between the system and the environment. The environment does not *determine* the structure of the system, but influences the development, as well as the transformation, reinforcement and stabilisation of patterns in the system.

In neural network terminology, the above distinction can be made in terms of supervised and unsupervised learning. The meaning of these terms will become clear in the process of analysing why both Changeaux and Edelman reject the first option. The rejection results from a denial of the idea that the world is pre-arranged in an informational fashion, i.e. of the idea that things are categorised in an *a priori* fashion, and that these categories can be known objectively. It is thus a rejection of that family of ideas that includes Platonism and logical positivism – the same family that forms the theoretical framework for classical AI.

One of the fundamental tasks of the nervous system is to carry on adaptive perceptual categorization in an 'unlabelled' world – one in which the macroscopic order and arrangement of objects and events (and even their definition or discrimination) cannot be prefigured for an organism, despite the fact that such objects and events obey the laws of physics.

(Edelman 1987: 7)

Any form of learning in which the system (here the nervous system) reflects the world *directly* implies some form of supervision – either by nature itself, which has to supply the categories and their labels, or by a homunculus. Edelman is explicit in rejecting these direct or 'informational' models, especially since they still form the backbone of most theories in cognitive science and artificial intelligence. It is worth quoting his analysis of these models at some length:

According to information processing models, neural signals from the periphery are encoded in a variety of ways and are subsequently transformed by various nuclei and way stations; finally, they are retransformed in a variety of ways by increasingly sophisticated relay systems culminating in cortical processing and output. Perforce, this view puts a very strong emphasis on strict rules for the generation of precise wiring during the development of the brain. . . . This view also makes an assumption about the nature of memory which it considers to occur by representation of events through recording or replication of their informational details.

(38)

It should be clear that the 'informational' approach depends heavily on the notion of predetermined structure – on abilities the system is 'born' with, rather than on abilities the system could acquire. Furthermore, it assumes a hierarchical, rule-based, representational model of the brain. This is not merely an assumption about the inner workings of the nervous system, but in fact a more basic ontological assumption about the fabric of the universe. It enacts a nostalgia to reduce the world to logical relationships that can be tracked down. It should come as no surprise that this approach is intimately linked to the rule-based approach to the modelling of complex systems, and Edelman is aware of that:

The notion of information processing tends to put a strong emphasis on the ability of the central nervous system to calculate the relevant invariance of a physical world. This view culminates in discussions of algorithms and computations, on the assumption that the brain computes in an algorithmic manner. . . . Categories of natural objects in the physical world are implicitly assumed to fall into defined classes or typologies that are accessible to a program. Pushing the notion even further, proponents of certain versions of this model are disposed to consider that the rules and representation (Chomsky 1980) that appear to emerge in the realization of syntactical structures and higher semantic functions of language arise from corresponding structures at the neural level. If statistical variation enters at all into such a view of the brain, it is considered in terms of noise in a signal, which in information processing models is taken to be the main manifestation of variation.

(38)

Edelman opposes the rule-based or informational view with 'population thinking' – his term for the distributed nature of complex systems. The next section will examine his approach in more detail.

Neural group selection

Edelman (1987) wishes to give an explanation of the higher functions of the brain, or more specifically, of how perceptual categorisation could occur, without making the assumption 'that the world is prearranged in an informational fashion or that the brain contains a homunculus' (4). His argument is therefore not based on the notion of the brain as consisting mainly of genetically predetermined structures, but rather of the brain as consisting of a large population of simple, undifferentiated but interconnected neurons. These neurons are dynamically organised into cellular groups with different structures and functions. To a large extent the organisation takes place during a development phase, but changes in this organisation do occur throughout the lifespan of the brain. The process depends on three principles (5):

- The homogeneous population of neurons is epigenetically diversified into structurally variant *groups* through a number of selective processes. A group consists of several neurons that have a strong connectivity to each other and a weak connectivity to other groups – connectivity being determined by the synapses. These groups form what Edelman calls the 'primary repertoire'.
- During the post-natal period the connections within and among groups are epigenetically modified through various signals received as a result of the interaction between the system and the environment. The structure of groups is refined and, more important, interaction (competition and co-operation) with other groups is brought about, leading to the establishment of functional groups likely to be used in future. They form the 'secondary repertoire'.
- Once the primary and secondary repertoires are in place, various groups interact by means of loops and feedback. This dynamic interaction is the result of a correlation of various sensory and motor responses which causes the formation of cortical maps that enable the brain to interpret conditions in its environment and act upon them. Numerous groups participate in map formation, and a specific group can be part of many maps.

We can summarise the model in the following general terms. The brain is pre-structured in a way that is general and non-specific, but with enough differentiation (i.e. enough asymmetry) to allow external influences a 'foothold'. The 'general' structure is then modified through experience and behaviour in order to reflect the specific circumstances encountered in the history of the organism in question. The brain thus organises itself so as to cope with its environment. Note that certain parts of the primary repertoire could be permanently 'hard-wired', and will therefore *not* be changed by experience. This enables the organism to transfer certain capabilities to its offspring genetically. Such capabilities would include the control of vital bodily functions necessary right from the start, as well as other capabilities the organism may need but does not have sufficient time to learn by itself. The beauty of the model is that both the hard-wired and the adaptive components are implemented in exactly the same way (i.e. as groups of neurons), denying any real distinction between the two.

Before turning to the process of map formation itself, two important and closely related characteristics of the model need discussion. In the first place, Edelman (1987) insists that the neural groups in the primary repertoire have to be 'degenerate' (6). This means that within the primary repertoire there are significant numbers of non-identical variant groups, each of which could eventually be associated with a certain input. There is nothing in the primary group that earmarks it for a specific function in an *a priori* way. In the second place, groups are not hermetic units, but are distributed over large overlapping areas (163). The notion of distributedness is an important one that, in the case of Edelman, is a direct result of taking the 'population' approach. Together these two characteristics – degeneracy and distributedness – deny the localisation of cortical function as well as the existence of hierarchical processing structures in a narrow sense (162).

Edelman discusses three important aspects of cortical map formation that elucidate the process of map formation and also incorporate some of the general principles of self-organisation. They are *group confinement, group selection* and *group competition*.

(i)   *Group confinement.* If the cortex consisted only of a homogeneous mass of neurons, it would have been impossible for any structure to develop. On the other hand, neurons by themselves are incapable of performing complex functions. Neural groups therefore have an optimum size, but unfortunately it is not constant or known *a priori*. The size has to be arrived at spontaneously and dynamically. In the cortex this is achieved by means of locally inhibitory connections in the horizontal plane, and locally excitatory connections vertically. Since the cortex is a thin sheet of neurons (crumpled up to fit into the cranium), activity is confined to groups orientated vertically, with less dense interaction in the horizontal plane. This ties in well with the known structure of the cortex, best visualised as lots of closely packed 'columns' (see Mountcastle 1978).

(ii)   *Group selection.* Group selection is mainly a function of the use-principle (Hebb's rule). The more a certain group is used, the more active it becomes. The process basically works in the following way. Bundles of nerves carrying impulses from some source (whether internal or external) activate certain neural groups. When the messages from more than one source overlap in a certain group, the correlation leads to a high level of activity in that group, and the neurons in that group will alter their synaptic strengths to become more sensitive to this correlation. After repeated exposure to a certain correlation, the group will respond to it strongly, and it is then said to be 'selected' for this correlation. Once selected, a group may well become active even if all the inputs are not present simultaneously. Consequently certain associations can be made and remembered. If the correlation occurs only irregularly, or is not strong enough, the synaptic modifications will fade away, and the group will again be available for selection by another process. To be able to forget remains a precondition for memory.

(iii)   *Group competition.* Once groups of the right size have been formed and selected, their stability is determined by their competitive interaction with other groups. Weak and small groups will be eliminated, and oversized or cumbersome groups will be divided and conquered by smaller, more vital groups – vitality being determined by the frequency and quality of stimulation and activity. Competition is also very sensitive to 'historical effects' (Edelman 1987: 165). The function of a group is determined by its history, and the functioning of extant groups can strongly influence the formation of new groups. By means of group competition, cortical maps are developed and maintained in a stable but dynamic fashion. Unused or unnecessary groups are eliminated, or 'cleared', without impairing the capacity for the development of new ones.

From these principles it can be seen that map formation not only provides a theory for the cognitive development of the brain, but also embodies the three basic characteristics of all self-organising systems: co-operation, competition and memory.

The relationship between the brain and the world

The basic characteristics of Edelman's model of the brain can now be summarised:

• Neural groups are formed in the network of the brain through a process of self-organisation.

- These groups are selected, altered and maintained in a dynamic way through interaction with the environment.
- Impulses (of internal or external origin) cause activity in certain groups, and through the activity of other related groups triggered in the process, appropriate responses can be generated.

A question that arises now is the following: in what way does the brain represent the necessary information about the environment? The purpose of the previous chapter was to argue that classical representation is not the appropriate mechanism, but here we have to say something more about the relationships between the environment and the structure of the brain.

It is important to point out that information from the environment influences the structure of the brain directly; it *causes* changes in the structure of the brain. However, the effect of these influences are not direct in the sense that the structure of the brain merely becomes a mirror of its environment. There are two reasons for this. In the first place the effects are *delayed*; the full impact of an external influence is not felt immediately. Since the system must have some resistance to change, the effects of the influence are taken up in a *process*, one that has always already begun and is never finally completed. In the second place, different impulses are always mixed as a result of the fact that the groups are embedded in a network. This means that although perception, for example, is a *direct* process – a certain impulse results in a direct response in the network – it does not remain *unmediated*.[9] Previous impulses (memory) as well as impulses from other sources co-operate in determining the nature of the response. The nature of the interaction between the neural system and the environment as discussed here can clearly be analysed in terms of Derrida's notion of *différance* (see Chapter 3).

A second aspect of interaction between the brain and its environment concerns the role of motor behaviour (Edelman 1987: 8, 45, 209–239). Map formation is not the result of brain processes only, since the available information is also determined by the way in which the organism actively explores its environment. The structure of the brain is strongly influenced by *action*. This supports the idea that intelligence is not an abstract process, but one that is embedded in the world. Our brains are part of our bodies (and vice versa).

The role of active motor behaviour forms the first half of the argument against abstract, solipsistic intelligence. The second half concerns the role of communication. The importance of communication, especially the use of symbol systems (language), does not return us to the paradigm of objective information-processing. Structures for communication remain embedded in a neural structure, and therefore will always be subjected to the complexities of network interaction. Our existence is both embodied and contingent.

PHILOSOPHICAL IMPLICATIONS OF SELF-ORGANISATION

Self-organisation is a specific characteristic of a number of real systems, i.e. systems that operate successfully in the world around us. It can be analysed in general terms and be given a mathematical description. The processes can furthermore be modelled and simulated on a computer, and can be used for solving problems. The insights gained in this way have important implications for our understanding of the world and its inhabitants. In this section a number of philosophical issues will be discussed.

The importance of relationships and patterns

Claiming that self-organisation is an important property of complex systems is to argue against foundationalism. The dynamic nature of self-organisation, where the structure of the system is continuously transformed through the interaction of contingent, external factors and historical, internal factors, cannot be explained by resorting to a single origin or to an immutable principle. In point of fact, self-organisation provides the mechanism whereby complex structure can evolve without having to postulate first beginnings or transcendental interventions. It is exactly in this sense that postmodern theory contributes to our understanding of complex, self-organising systems.

For reasons similar to the above, self-organising systems are also anti-reductionistic. As a result of the complex patterns of interaction, the behaviour of a system cannot be explained solely in terms of its atomistic components, despite the fact that the system does not consist of anything else but the basic components and their interconnections. Complex characteristics 'emerge' through the process of interaction within the system. Garfinkel (1987: 202–203) discusses the relationships between parts and whole in a biological context:

> We have seen that modeling aggregation requires us to transcend the level of the individual cells to describe the system by holistic variables. But in classical reductionism, the behavior of holistic entities must ultimately be explained by reference to the nature of their constituents, because those entities 'are just' collections of the lower-level objects with their interactions. Although it may be true in some sense that systems 'are just' collections of their elements, it does not follow that we can *explain* the system's behaviour by reference to its parts, together with a theory of their connections. In particular, in dealing with systems of large numbers of similar components, we must make recourse to holistic concepts that refer to the behavior of the system as a whole. We have seen here, for example, concepts such as entrainment, global attractors, waves of aggregation, and so on. Although these system properties must ultimately be definable in terms of the states of individuals, this fact does not make them 'fictions'; they are causally efficacious (hence, *real*) and have definite

causal relationships with other system variables and even to the states of the individuals.

The relevance of self-organisation becomes clear upon the adoption of a certain kind of systems thinking that attempts to incorporate and include rather than to falsify and ignore. It is a kind of thinking that is not horrified by contradictions and opposites but rather turns them into the forces that vitalise the system. Variations of systems thinking have been with us since the dawn of philosophy. The position of Heraclitus provides a good example. For him, the basic principle of the universe was strife: war is common to all and strife is justice, and all things come into being and pass away through strife. Instead of privileging a specific element – as Thales did with water and Anaximenes with air – Heraclitus placed everything in mutual *competition*. In this dynamic tension 'all things come into being and pass away'. A kind of systems thinking also governs the medieval theories concerning the four elements and their respective humours and principles (Flanagan 1990: 80–105; Wilden 1987: 151–166). The ideal state of affairs occurs when all the elements are in balance, when they co-operate. This harmony was believed to be unobtainable in the fallen state of the world and therefore constant adjustment is necessary. Modern examples of systems thinking would include the linguistics of Saussure and Freudian psychology. The postmodern denial of single meta-narratives, and its emphasis on the importance of difference and opposition, is not normally formulated in terms of 'population thinking' (to use the biological expression for the kind of systems thinking referred to here), but the similarities are undeniable.

Although strains of thought that value the importance of relationships – and look for patterns rather than essences – can be found throughout the intellectual history of the West, they have usually been trampled over by more macho theories claiming to have found the Truth: Platonic idealism, rationalism, Marxism, positivism. In our analysis of complex systems (like the brain and language) we must avoid the trap of trying to find master keys. Because of the mechanisms by which complex systems structure themselves, single principles provide inadequate descriptions. We should rather be sensitive to complex and self-organising interactions and appreciate the play of patterns that perpetually transforms the system itself as well as the environment in which it operates.

The role of history

The important role played by memory in self-organising systems has been mentioned frequently, but the topic deserves another brief discussion in a philosophical context.[10] No complex system, whether biological or social, can be understood without considering its history. Two similar systems placed in identical conditions may respond in vastly different ways if they have different histories. To be more precise, the history of a system is not merely important in the *understanding* of the system, it co-determines the *structure* of the system.

The notion of history, however, should be used with care when analysing a system. It should not be seen as providing a key to final descriptions of a system. This is because the history of a system is not present in the system in such a way that it can be reconstructed. The 'effects' of the history of the system are important, but the history itself is continuously transformed through self-organising processes in the system – only the traces of history remain, distributed through the system. These traces, modelled in a neural network by the interconnections and their 'weights', do not correspond to facts, ideas or symbols, since they encode information at an extremely low level. Global behaviour of the system is the result of *'patterns* of traces' – the individual traces that constitute the pattern have no meaning by themselves. Individual traces can belong to more than one pattern and the same pattern is not always constituted by the same collection of traces. Since the traces are perpetually transformed, it is not possible, strictly speaking, to ever have exactly the 'same' pattern again. Any complex, dynamic system is continuously transformed by both its environment and itself.

The same arguments hold for memory in the context of the brain. Memories are not stored in the brain as discrete units that can be recalled as if from a filing cabinet. Memory traces are stored in a distributed fashion and are continuously altered by experience. In a manner of speaking, even though memory is the substrate for all the brain's higher functions, there are no 'memories'. This follows from the notion of 'distributed representation'. The fact that information is 'smeared' over many units is a vital characteristic of complex systems, not a mere alternative to iconic representation.

Active and passive

Another philosophically important aspect of self-organisation is that the process is somehow suspended between the active and passive modes.[11] A self-organising system reacts to the state of affairs in the environment, but simultaneously transforms itself as a result of these affairs, often affecting the environment in turn. Processes in the system are therefore neither simply passive reflections of the outside, nor are they actively determined from the inside. The very distinction between active and passive, as well as that between inside and outside, comes under pressure. In a complex system, control does not emanate from a single source. Should this happen, the system would become degenerate, lose its adaptability and survive only as long as the environment remained stable. These notions have implications for the way we think about social systems, an issue that will be turned to towards the end of the chapter.

Another aspect of self-organisation, closely related to the suspension between active and passive, is the reflexivity of the process. Self-organisation is a self-transforming process; the system acts upon itself. Reflexivity disallows any static description of the system since it is not possible to intercept the reflexive moment. It also disallows a complete description of the system at a meta-level (Lawson 1985: 20, 21). A meta-level can always be *constructed*, but from such a perspective only snapshots of the system as it exists at a given moment will be possible, i.e. frozen moments that do not incorporate the residues of the past or the shadows of the future. The temporal complexities produced by the reflexive nature of self-organising systems cannot be represented.[12]

Our understanding of complex systems cannot ignore the role of reflexivity or the mode of operation suspended between active and passive. These aspects do, however, create serious difficulties when attempts are made to model complex systems. The present limitations of formal models do not preclude the possibility of constructing 'machines' that would incorporate the salient characteristics of complex systems, but one should bear in mind that such machines will be as complex as the systems they model and therefore they will be equally difficult to analyse. A complex neural network may be an example of such a 'machine'.

Stability and prediction

In the discussion of self-organised criticality the necessity for a delicate balance between order and disorder was underscored. Similar considerations hold when analysing the stability of a system, or when trying to predict its behaviour.

The classical definition of stability states that in a stable system small causes produce small effects. In a critically organised system this is not the case, and by classical considerations it would have to be called unstable. Unfortunately, as far as living complex systems are concerned, classical stability would amount to stagnation and death. A reinterpretation of the notion of 'stability' is thus called for.

The classical definition of *instability*, at least as used by Poincaré, is probabilistic. Unstable events are defined as events that have no observable cause (Pattee 1987: 328). They are thus chance events, as opposed to deterministic ones. In complex systems, however, novel, unpredicted behaviour need not be a result of chance. It can be 'caused' by the complex interaction of a large number of factors – factors that may not be logically compatible. Complexity is not to be confused with randomness and chance, but cannot be described in first-order logical terms either. 'I find no alternative but to accept multiple, formally incompatible descriptions as a satisfactory explanation of many types of biological events' (Pattee 1987: 329). It is the interaction of complex constraints that produces interesting behaviour – behaviour that cannot be described as chance events or instabilities. A theory based on chance events, including those of quantum theory, 'serves only as an escape from classical determinism: it is not a theory of self-organization' (Pattee 1987: 330).

This brings us to the question of prediction. To be able to predict the behaviour of a system is one of the classic criteria for a successful theory. We are working with systems, however, that cannot be fully described by means of a classical theory. Predicting their behaviour can be very problematic. The problems involved are described by Krohn and Küppers (1989: 155, 156):

> In the case of these 'complex systems' (Nicolis and Prigogine [1989]), or 'non-trivial machines' (von Foerster 1985), a functional analysis of input–output correlations must be supplemented by the study of the 'mechanisms', i.e. by causal analysis. Due to the operational conditions of complex systems it is almost impossible to make sense of the output (in terms of functions or expected effects) without taking into account the mechanisms by which it is produced. The output of the system follows the 'history' of the system, which itself depends on its previous output taken as input (operational closure). The system's development is determined by its mechanisms, but cannot be predicted, because no reliable rule can be found in the output itself. Even more complicated are systems in which the working mechanisms themselves can develop according to recursive operations (learning of learning; invention of invention, etc.).

With the help of a mapping of the major constraints pertaining to a system and some knowledge about the history and environment of the system, predictions can be attempted, but never with certainty. Considerations such as these are of practical importance to many social systems forced to cope with complex environments. Examples would include political groups in turbulent times, research establishments that have to compete for limited funds, and commercial organisations in a fluctuating economy. Since the certainty with which the future can be predicted has been greatly reduced, any plan of action has to be adapted continuously. If the plan is too rigid – too much central control – the system will not be able to cope with unpredictable changes. On the other hand, it will also be disastrous if the system tries to adjust itself to every superficial change, since such changes may easily be reversed without notice. The system will waste its resources in trying to follow every fluctuation instead of adapting to higher-order trends. Being able to discriminate between changes that should be followed and changes that should be resisted is vital to the survival of any organisation (or organism). This is achieved optimally when the control of the system is not rigid and localised, but distributed over the system, ensuring that the positive dynamics of self-organisation is utilised effectively.

Finally, we can consider some of the implications the process of self-organisation has for ethics.

The ethics of self-organisation

A traditional criticism of evolution, and by extension also of self-organisation, is that it provides us with too mechanistic a view of human existence. Human beings, this critique claims, cannot be understood merely in terms of a tooth-and-claw existence. Our existence is also governed by values that give meaning to life. Such a critique is of course only possible on the basis of some metaphysical commitments – on the basis either of religion, or of some universal, abstract (Kantian) principle – and is closely related to the position that claims that there is no such thing as postmodern ethics.

Does a theory of self-organisation claim that it is possible to describe human behaviour without recourse to a general system of values? If this question refers to values that are separate from, or prior to, the contingency of our existence, the answer has to be yes. There is, however, another understanding of values which is not only compatible with a theory of self-organisation, but which can be viewed as a result of it. In this view, values are understood as emergent properties of the social system. I will give two examples.

- The modelling of evolutionary (or self-organising) systems has shown that purely selfish behaviour by members of a system is detrimental not only to the system, but ultimately also to the particular individuals. Altruistic behaviour is therefore not a 'value' adopted by 'nice' individuals; it is a characteristic necessary for the survival and flourishing of a system (see Axelrod 1984).
- We have seen that distributed, decentralised control makes a system more flexible, and therefore increases its survivability. If we apply this notion to social systems, it would seem that we have an argument against rigid, centralised control mechanisms in, for example, the management of a company or the running of a state. Once again, this kind of critique against autocratic management or a fascist government is based not on the idea that these things are 'bad' *per se*, but rather on the knowledge that they will ultimately lead to the degeneration of the system in question.

Do these properties imply an ethics of self-organisation? I would be very hesitant to use the word 'ethics' here, unless it is an ethics in the sense of 'principles that *constitute* a system', closer to the way in which Levinas would use the term. It is certainly quite far removed from the norms of public morality. The significance of these notions will be explored in greater detail in the final chapter.

7 Complexity and postmodernism

ACKNOWLEDGING COMPLEXITY

Whether or not we are happy with calling the times we live in 'postmodern', there is no denying that the world we live in is complex and that we have to confront this complexity if we are to survive, and, perhaps, even prosper. The traditional (or modern) way of confronting complexity was to find a secure point of reference that could serve as foundation, a passe-partout, a master key from which everything else could be derived. Whatever that point of reference might be – a transcendental world of perfect ideas, the radically sceptic mind, the phenomenological subject – my claim is that following such a strategy constitutes an *avoidance* of complexity. The obsession to find one essential truth blinds us to the relationary nature of complexity, and especially to the continuous shifting of those relationships. Any acknowledgement of complexity will have to incorporate these shifts and changes, not as epiphenomena, but as *constitutive* of complex systems.

In this study we have so far concerned ourselves with the development of an understanding of complexity at a fairly technical level. In the process we have continuously opposed two approaches – the formal, rule-based, representational one and the distributed, self-organising, connectionist one. The general conclusion has been that the rule-based approach is not sensitive enough to the general characteristics of complex systems. It has been argued that connectionist models fare somewhat better since they are implicitly sensitive to the relational character of complex systems, perhaps as a result of the fact that they are based on the best example of a complex system we know – the brain. Even though their capabilities may at present be nowhere near those of the mammalian brain, they at least incorporate some of the general characteristics of complex systems.

In this chapter I wish to argue that an acknowledgement of complexity can assist us when confronting a number of important philosophical issues, including ethical and political ones. I will analyse the relationships between relational models of complexity and postmodernism. An argument will be presented against the view that a postmodern approach implies that 'anything goes'. Instead, the suggestion will be that the postmodern approach is inherently sensitive to complexity, that it acknowledges the importance of self-organisation whilst denying a conventional theory of representation. The focus will be on a *locus classicus* of postmodern theory: Jean-François Lyotard's *The Postmodern Condition*. I will also look at some of the implications this characterisation of complexity has for our understanding of language, social theory, the status of our knowledge claims, and ethics.

POSTMODERNISM

The word 'postmodern' has acquired so many different meanings that it has become impossible to define it. Literature on postmodernism has proliferated to such an extent that it has become difficult to know exactly what position it is that one has to engage with. Sometimes the terms 'postmodern' and 'post-structural' are conflated, at other times a clear distinction is made between them; sometimes 'postmodern' is used as a rigorous theoretical term, at other times it is used as a vague term describing the contemporary cultural scene. In order to provide some focus, I will concentrate on a classical text in this field, *The Postmodern Condition* (Lyotard 1984). The choice is motivated by the fact that my interest here is in the status of postmodern *knowledge,* and not in a general cultural survey. I also have no intention to provide an apology for postmodernism, or some specific interpretation thereof, but rather wish to analyse contemporary society and social theory in terms of our conceptual models of complexity. I will argue that the proliferation of discourses and meaning described in postmodern theory is not created by wilful and disruptive theorists, but that it is an inescapable effect of the complexities of our linguistic and social spaces. The proliferation of information as well as the way in which the media collapse international public space into local private space prevent us from coming up with unifying, coherent descriptions of our world.

It is along these lines that Lyotard develops his description of postmodernism. His aim is to study the conditions of knowledge in developed societies (xxiii). Scientific knowledge, he claims, habitually legitimates itself by appealing to a coherent metadiscourse that performs a general unifying function. Should such a metadiscourse be found, it will be possible to incorporate all forms of knowledge into one grand narrative. This is the dream of modernism.

> I will use the term *modern* to designate any science that legitimates itself with reference to a metadiscourse of this kind making explicit appeal to some grand narrative, such as the dialectics of the Spirit, the hermeneutics of meaning, the emancipation of the rational or working subject, or the creation of wealth.
>
> (xxiii)

Postmodernism is consequently defined as 'incredulity towards meta-narratives' (xxiv). Instead of looking for a simple discourse that can unify all forms of knowledge, we have to cope with a multiplicity of discourses, many different language games – all of which are determined locally, not legitimated externally. Different institutions and different contexts produce different narratives which are not reducible to each other.

> The narrative function is losing its functors, its great hero, its great voyages, its great goal. It is being dispersed in clouds of narrative language elements – narrative, but also denotative, prescriptive, descriptive, and so on. Conveyed within each cloud are pragmatic valencies specific to its kind. Each of us lives at the intersection of many of these. However, we do not necessarily establish stable language combinations, and the properties of the ones we do establish are not necessarily communicable.
>
> (xxiv)

This description of knowledge as the outcome of a multiplicity of local narratives, it must be stressed, is an argument not against scientific knowledge as such, but against a certain *understanding* of such knowledge. Lyotard rejects an interpretation of science as representing the totality of all true knowledge. He argues for a narrative understanding of knowledge, portraying it as a plurality of smaller stories that function well within the particular contexts where they apply (7). Instead of claiming the impossibility of knowledge, 'it refines our sensitivity to differences and reinforces our ability to tolerate the incommensurable. Its principle is not the expert's homology, but the inventor's paralogy' (xxv).[1]

Let me summarise Lyotard's position. Different groups (institutions, disciplines, communities) tell different stories about what they know and what they do. Their knowledge does not take the form of a logically structured and complete whole, but rather takes the form of narratives that are instrumental in allowing them to achieve their goals and to make sense of what they are doing. Since these narratives are all local, they cannot be linked together to form a grand narrative which unifies all knowledge. The postmodern condition is characterised by the co-existence of a multiplicity of heterogeneous discourses – a state of affairs assessed differently by different parties. Those who have a nostalgia for a unifying metanarrative – a dream central to the history of Western metaphysics – experience the postmodern condition as fragmented, full of anarchy and therefore ultimately meaningless. It leaves them with a feeling of vertigo. On the other hand, those who embrace postmodernism find it challenging, exciting and full of uncharted spaces. It fills them with a sense of adventure. Which of these two evaluations apply is often determined by whether one feels comfortable without fixed points of reference. The choice between the two is determined by psychological just as much as theoretical considerations. In the present study, however, I will confine myself to theoretical issues.

There is one important argument often used against postmodernism (see e.g. Parushnikova 1992). It claims that if all narratives were to have only local legitimation, the resulting fragmentation of the social fabric would relativise *all* knowledge. Since there is no external 'check' on any discourse, no local narratives can be seriously criticised. Each discourse will become independent of all others, leading to the closure and isolation of discursive communities. Ultimately it would imply that each individual has only herself as a point of reference with no way of grounding any knowledge objectively. The outcome would be a situation where 'anything goes' – a position that is clearly unacceptable, especially within the context of the philosophy of science.

The general argument against postmodernism – that the denial of fixed points of reference implies that anything goes – is, to my mind at least, fallacious. It is equivalent to saying that if the sun does not shine, it must be dark. I wish to argue that, at least as far as Lyotard is concerned, postmodernism need not entail a position of 'anything goes'. The 'anything goes' argument depends on a certain understanding of the role of the individual, one that is explicitly rejected by Lyotard (1984: 15).[2]

> This breaking up of the grand Narratives . . . leads to what some authors analyze in terms of the dissolution of the social bond and the disintegration of social aggregates into a mass of individual atoms thrown into the absurdity of Brownian motion. Nothing of the kind is happening: this point of view, it seems to me, is haunted by the paradisaic representation of a lost 'organic' society.

To proponents of the 'anything goes' position, a *rejection* of an understanding of the individual as an isolated, autonomous agent with a 'natural' role in an 'organic' whole is synonymous with an *acceptance* of a fragmented, atomistic view of the individual. A careful reading of Lyotard shows that his understanding of the individual is formulated in such a way as to *counter* the idea of fragmentation and isolation that could result from a dismissal of the grand narrative. The following quotation contains a number of important points that will be analysed closely. It also illuminates the relationships between Lyotard's model of postmodern society and the connectionist model developed in this study (including the characteristics of self-organisation and distributed representation).

> A *self* does not amount to much, but no self is an island; each exists in a fabric of relations that is now more complex and mobile than ever before. Young or old, man or woman, rich or poor, a person is always located at 'nodal points' of specific communication circuits, however tiny these may be. Or better: one is always located at a post through which various kinds of messages pass. No one, not even the least privileged among us, is ever entirely powerless over the messages that traverse and position him at the post of sender, addressee, or referent. One's mobility in relation to these

language game effects (language games, of course, are what this is all about) is tolerable, at least within certain limits (and the limits are vague); it is even solicited by regulatory mechanisms, and in particular by the self-adjustments the system undertakes in order to improve its performance. It may even be said that the system can and must encourage such movement to the extent that it combats its own entropy; the novelty of an unexpected 'move', with its correlative displacement of a partner or group of partners, can supply the system with that increased performativity it forever demands and consumes.

(15)

The relevance of the connectionist model is clearly indicated by this passage. The self is understood in terms of a 'fabric of relations', a node in a network, and not in terms of atomistic units standing by and for themselves. Since it is the relationships that are important, and not the node as such, 'a self does not amount to much'. Lyotard's description of the postmodern condition is in fact a description of the network of our society and of the manner in which it produces and reproduces knowledge. His point is that this network has become too complex for general or overarching descriptions. All the characteristics of a complex system (as described in Chapter 1) can be found in it – something to be discussed presently. The argument for a multiplicity of discourses is not a wilful move; it is an acknowledgement of complexity. It allows for the explosion of information and the inevitable contradictions that form part of a truly complex network.

The critique claiming that a postmodern position would produce many isolated discourses in which anything goes is countered in two ways. In the first place, society forms a network. Although different discourses form 'clusters' within this network, they cannot isolate themselves from the network. There are always connections to other discourses. The different local narratives interact, some more than others, but no discourse is fixed or stabilised by itself. Different discourses – clusters in the network – may grow, shrink, break up, coalesce, absorb others or be absorbed. Local narratives only make sense in terms of their contrasts and differences to surrounding narratives. What we have is a self-organising process in which meaning is generated through a dynamic process, and not through the passive reflection of an autonomous agent that can make 'anything go'. Instead of being self-sufficient and isolated, discourses are in constant interaction, battling with each other for territory, the provisional boundaries between them being the very stakes in the game. This is what Lyotard calls 'the agonistic aspects of society' (16–17).

The second aspect of the network of society that counters the idea of isolation is the distributed nature of the network. In a connectionist network information is not 'represented' by specific nodes, but encoded in patterns distributed over many nodes. Conversely, any specific node forms part of many different patterns. In the social network, discourses are similarly spread over many 'selves'. A discourse is merely a 'pattern of activity' over a large group of individuals exchanging local information, and does not represent any aspect of a metanarrative. Each individual is also part of many patterns. One can be a mother, a scientist, a consumer, a political activist, an artist and a lover, all at the same time. Since the social network shares the characteristic of distributedness with connectionist networks, the argument claiming that postmodernism results in *isolation* misses the target completely.

A further aspect of the social network Lyotard refers to in the passage cited above is that of self-organisation – the 'self-adjustments the system undertakes to improve its own performance'. I have already pointed to the fact that the discarding of a determining metanarrative on the one hand, and of the autonomous agent on the other, suspends the self-organising process somewhere between active and passive modes. The dynamics of the social network also share the other characteristics of self-organisation discussed in the previous chapter. The social fabric is not 'designed' by means of some transcendental principle, but develops as a result of the way in which it responds to contingent information in a dynamic fashion. The process is a complex one involving many individuals with complex, non-linear relationships between them, including feedback relations. Individuals co-operate to form clusters, but also compete for resources in the network. The system is therefore not, and can never be, symmetrical (a point we will return to). The *history* of the system is vitally important for the way in which meaning is generated in any part of it. The evolution of structures in the social fabric, causing continuous alterations, is an integral part of its dynamics.

Lyotard is quite clear on the point that the complexity of the social system does *not* automatically lead to randomness or noise. From the passage above it is clear that the system 'combats entropy', that it generates meaning, not noise or chaos. To optimise this process, the system has to be as diverse as possible, not as structured as possible. This, for Lyotard, is the function of paralogy. Paralogy thus performs a similar function to that of self-organised criticality (discussed in the previous chapter).

Self-organised criticality is the mechanism by which networks diversify their internal structure maximally. The more diverse the structure, the richer is the information that can be stored and manipulated. The network has to walk the tightrope between solid structure, on the one hand, and disorder, on the other. In our network model, this process is the consequence of fierce competition among units or groups of units. For Lyotard, the driving force in a social system is that of paralogy and dissension:

> . . . it is now dissension that must be emphasized. Consensus is a horizon that is never reached. Research that takes place under the aegis of a paradigm tends to stabilize; it is like the exploitation of a technological, economic, or artistic 'idea'. It cannot be discounted. But what is striking

is that someone always comes along to disturb the order of 'reason'. It is necessary to posit the existence of a power that destabilizes the capacity for explanation, manifested in the promulgation of new norms for understanding or, if one prefers, in a proposal to establish new rules circumscribing a new field of research for the language of science.

(61)

Lyotard's insistence on dissension and destabilising forces, as opposed to consensus – notions which also form the core of Lyotard's critique of Habermas – has serious implications for philosophy in general, and specifically for the philosophy of science. The role of science has traditionally been understood as one that has to fix knowledge in a permanent grid. Experimental evidence was used to verify theories. Sufficient verification would ensure a permanent place in the grid. It soon became clear, however, that the conditions for objective verification were problematic, that experimental evidence could *support* a theory, but not *prove* it. The experimental process cannot include all the factors that could possibly be involved, nor can it predict how new knowledge would change the interpretation of experimental results. Since one could still *disprove* theories, the process of verification was replaced by one of falsification. If one could not add to the grid, one could at least disqualify unwanted members. This strategy of 'throwing away' has the result of making the body of knowledge qualifying as 'scientific' leaner and leaner. Everything too complex or containing uncertainties or unpredictability is, for the time being at least, left aside. Consequently, large parts of the totality of human knowledge are disregarded as unscientific – most of the arts, most of psychology (for many scientists Freud remains the paradigm of a scientific charlatan), and often, human sciences in general. Working with a narrow understanding of what science should be, even the life sciences (biology) and the empirical sciences (engineering) become suspect. Pushed to its limits; the theory of falsification implies that only abstract, *a priori* truths are really scientific.

Lyotard's suggestion is that we discard the idea of consensus since it is impoverishing. To proliferate knowledge, we have to proliferate discourses without trying to fix them into a permanent grid. This position has some affinity with the position of Paul Feyerabend (1975). Feyerabend insists on a scientific 'anarchy' in which all the marginalised voices should participate. There should be no immutable 'method' that determines what forms part of the canon and what does not. Instead of throwing away everything that does not fit into the scheme, one should try to find meaningful relationships among the different discourses.

In this regard the connectionist model provides us with an extremely important insight. If it is granted that all knowledge is embedded in the larger social network – the acceptance of this point remains a kind of watershed – the proliferation of meaning and discourses is an inevitable characteristic of a complex, self-organising network. Lyotard and

Feyerabend are not wilfully disruptive, anti-scientific anarchists; they are considering the conditions of knowledge in a complex society. To allow previously marginalised voices equal opportunity once again does not imply that 'anything goes'. Dissenting voices receive no special privilege; they have to enter into the 'agonistics of the network', where their relevance is dynamically determined through competition and co-operation in terms of the history as well as the changing needs and goals of the system.

To conclude this section, a cautionary note. Since all the networks we have talked about are contingent entities, they are finite. Even the most complex ones have a finite capacity for handling information. A network can therefore suffer from an overload, especially when confronted with too much novelty. An overloaded network will show 'pathological' behaviour, either in terms of chaotic behaviour or in terms of catatonic shutdown. This may actually be the state of affairs many critics of postmodernism fear, one in which we are being overloaded with information and, in the process, annihilated (e.g. Baudrillard 1988). The point is, however, that there is little escape. Reverting to rigid, central control or the reintroduction of grand narratives will not make the information go away. We have to learn to cope with it by being more discriminating, by filtering out some of the excesses.

Once again, the connectionist model is the most effective one for performing this 'filtering'. In a rule-based system, preferences have to be programmed in, and can be adjusted only with difficulty. Such systems remain paradigmatic of the modernist approach working with abstract forms of meaning (representation) and central control. Connectionist models can dynamically adjust themselves in order to select that which is to be inhibited and that which is to be enhanced. Robustness and flexibility are two sides of the same coin. In terms of our social condition, this means that we would experience less postmodern stress by becoming less rigid in our interaction with each other and our environment. This does not mean that one should give up, or go with the flow. It means that we all have to enter into the agonistics of the network.

COMPLEX SYSTEMS AND POSTMODERN SOCIETY

In this section I wish to argue that postmodern society (seen as a system) can be described in terms of the ten characteristics of complex systems described in Chapter 1. I will take them one by one and argue that some of them have interesting implications for a theory of contemporary culture.

(i)   *Complex systems consist of a large number of elements.* If we look at the social system as constituted by human individuals, the number of elements in the system is certainly huge.

(ii) *The elements in a complex system interact dynamically.* Individuals are engaged in a constant exchange of information. Remember that a specific node in a neural network has limited significance, that it is the patterns of interconnections that encode information and generate meaning. Similarly, no human individual's existence is meaningful in isolation: 'the self does not amount to much' (Lyotard 1984: 15). The individual is constituted by its relationships to others.

(iii) *The level of interaction is fairly rich.* Human individuals interact with many others in a vast array of different capacities. In postmodern society the level of interaction is growing continuously.

(iv) *Interactions are non-linear.* Non-linearity is a precondition for complexity, especially where self-organisation, dynamic adaptation and evolution are at stake. Closely related to the principle of non-linearity is the principle of asymmetry. Linear, symmetrical relationships give rise to simple systems with transparent structures. In complex systems, mechanisms have to be found to break symmetry and to exploit the magnifying power of non-linearity. This is ensured by a rich level of interaction and by the competition for resources.

The social system is non-linear and asymmetrical as well. The same piece of information has different effects on different individuals, and small causes can have large effects. The competitive nature of social systems is often regulated by relations of power, ensuring an asymmetrical system of relationships. This, it must be emphasised strongly, is not an argument in favour of relations of *domination* or exploitation. The argument is merely one for the acknowledgement of complexity. Non-linearity, asymmetry, power and competition are inevitable components of complex systems. It is what keeps them going, their engine. If there were a symmetrical relationship between infants and adults, infants would never survive. If there were a symmetrical relationship between teacher and student, the student would never learn anything new. If the state had no power, it would have no reason to exist. If women and men were all the same, our world would be infinitely less interesting.

These considerations have important implications for social theory. The fact that society is held together by asymmetrical relations of power does not mean that these relationships are never exploited. To the contrary, they are continuously exploited by parents, by lecturers, by the state and by men, but also by children, by students, by citizens and by women. The point is that the solution to these forms of exploitation does not lie in some symmetrical space where power is distributed evenly. Such spaces cannot exist in complex systems that are driven by non-linearity. The hope that such spaces could be created in any enduring fashion is false.[3] To combat exploitation, there is only one option: you have to enter into the agonistics of the network. Since this approach does in no way guarantee success, there is very little moral high ground to be had, whether one rejects the abstract rules of modernist ethics or not.

(v)   *The interactions have a fairly short range.* The elements in a complex network usually interact primarily with those around them. In large networks this results in groups or assemblies of elements clustering together to perform more specific functions. Lyotard (1984: xxiv, 61, 66) describes the phenomenon as 'local determination'. Elements operate on information that is available to them locally – they have to, since in the complex (postmodern) system there is no meta-level controlling the flow of information. The behaviour of the system is therefore characterised best in terms of a multiplicity of local 'discourses'.

At the risk of repetition, it must be emphasised that these locally determined groups are *not* isolated from each other. Despite the short range of immediate interactions, nothing precludes wide-ranging *influence*. Different clusters are interconnected and since these connections are non-linear, they can produce large effects, even if the interconnections are sparse. Important events can reverberate through the system quite rapidly, but they are never propagated in a pure form since they are constantly modulated by the cluster they pass through.

(vi) *There are loops in the interconnections.* Feedback is an essential aspect of complex systems. Not feedback as understood simply in terms of control theory, but as intricately interlinked loops in a large network. This means that the activity of an element can directly or indirectly influence itself. In postmodern theory this manifests itself as the problem of reflexivity (see Lawson 1985). If one accepts that information is proliferated throughout the system and that it is continually transformed – by other bits of information and by itself – then it becomes impossible to stipulate a 'true' interpretation for any piece of information. Information can only be interpreted locally and then only through the dynamics of *différance* – as reflecting upon and transforming itself. These dynamics precludes the definition of truth or origin at a meta-level and is therefore referred to as the postmodern predicament – 'a crisis of our truths, our values, our most cherished beliefs' (Lawson 1985: 9).

There may indeed be a crisis of knowledge, but, and this must be underscored, the crisis is not the result of the disruptive activity of 'subversive' theoreticians like Nietzsche, Heidegger and Derrida. It is a direct result of the complexity of our postmodern society. This is the point Lyotard also makes when he insists that the *conditions* for knowledge are locally determined. Reflexivity does lead to paradox, but this is only a problem if all paradox has to be resolved at a meta-level. If one has to remain at the level of the network, one has to cope with the paralogy of the postmodern condition. The implication is *not* that it is impossible to interpret information; it merely means that all interpretations are contingent and provisional, pertaining to a certain context and a certain time-frame.

(vii)   *Complex systems are open systems.* We already made the point that local discourses are not closed off, but interact with each other. The social system also interacts with many other systems, including, for example, the ecosystem. This relationship has come under new scrutiny, giving rise to strong political groupings with the environment as their prime concern. Nature is no longer the passive object of human exploitation, but is part of the set of relationships that makes humans what they are.

(viii)   *Complex systems operate under conditions far from equilibrium.* Complex systems need a constant flow of energy to change, evolve and survive as complex entities. Equilibrium, symmetry and complete stability mean death. Just as the *flow* of energy is necessary to fight entropy and maintain the complex structure of the system, society can only survive as a *process*. It is defined not by its origins or its goals, but by what it is doing. In postmodern society this constant activity, this lack of equilibrium, is pushed to ever higher levels, particularly through the role of the mass media. This has an unsettling effect on many, and undeniably one has to develop certain skills to cope with these conditions, but to yearn for a state of complete equilibrium is to yearn for a sarcophagus.

(ix)   *Complex systems have histories.* The importance of history has been emphasised over and over again. One point bears repetition: the history of a complex system is not an objectively given state; it is a collection of traces distributed over the system, and is always open to multiple interpretations. History, understood in this sense, certainly applies to postmodern society, making it all but a-historical. What postmodernism does reject is an interpretation of history which elevates it to a master key for unlocking the true meaning of present conditions. However, it remains impossible to think in the present without considering the past – or the future.

(x)   *Individual elements are ignorant of the behaviour of the whole system in which they are embedded.* This is a more complex point that needs careful consideration. We have already pointed to the fact that elements in a system can only respond to local information, bearing in mind that this information can be quite rich. We have also shown that single elements of a complex system are not significant by themselves, but obtain significance through their patterns of interaction. The point made here is slightly different. Single elements cannot contain the complexity of the whole system and can therefore neither control nor comprehend it fully.

Because of the overwhelming amount of information available in postmodern society, we often live under the illusion that we get the complete picture. Because of the complexity of our society, this is not possible. Since we are in part creating society through our actions, no complete picture of its present state is available to anyone. In this regard all elements are in the same boat. Certain elements may have more control over specific aspects – our political models are still geared in a way that allows single individuals far too much power. Single elements should not, and normally do not, exert complete control over a decentralised system. For example, I may want to combat inflation, but I have no way of measuring the effect of my own spending pattern. These effects only become apparent when my behaviour combines with those of a large number of other economic agents.

The claim that the structure of society is an emergent property of the social system may create a feeling that one's own activities are irrelevant or insignificant. This need not be the case. In the first place, the relevance of your activities is determined by the effectiveness with which you enter into the agonistics of the network, not by attempts to understand life from God's viewpoint. Secondly, it must be kept in mind that since the interactions are non-linear, small causes can have large effects. It also means, however, that the effects of our actions are somewhat unpredictable.

Looking at these ten characteristics should make it clear that it is possible to analyse postmodern society in terms of the distributed model of complex systems. What is of particular interest is the implications the model seems to have for ethics. These will be dealt with towards the end of the chapter. In the following sections I want to look at the implications the model has for our understanding of language, and for the status of scientific knowledge.

LANGUAGE AS A COMPLEX SYSTEM

In Chapter 2 I outlined two paradigmatic approaches to language: the rule-based approach of Chomsky and the relational approach of Saussure. I argued for the affinities between connectionist models and Saussurian linguistics, and also discussed how complex networks can incorporate some of Derrida's expansions and critiques of Saussure (discussed in Chapter 3). In Chapter 5 the problem of representation was analysed, with specific reference to representational theories of meaning. Language has therefore already received a great deal of attention. In this section I want to summarise the implications the distributed model of complex systems has for the theory of language. To really characterise language in these terms, and to evaluate various theories of language against this background, would demand a full-length study of its own. To then develop a full-fledged connectionist model of language and to test it computationally would be an equally daunting task. Here I merely want to indicate why such a project would be meaningful.

Similar to the way in which postmodern society was shown to have the important characteristics of complex systems, we can examine language in order to establish to what extent the model applies to it as well. Since we have been through the exercise once before, I will move a little faster. Any proper language consists of a large number of words whose meanings are constituted through their relationships to each other (this is within the Saussurian paradigm, of course). In these relationships non-linearity and asymmetry are of vital importance. For example, while the meaning of 'red' is constituted through a set of relationships to all the other words in the system, its relationships to 'blue' and 'yellow' are not similar to its relationships to 'blood' or 'materialism'. The asymmetry of linguistic relationships is also a precondition for the development of metaphor. To say that *A* is a *B* (he is a pig) does *not* imply that *B* is an *A*. However, most terms are primarily constituted by their relationships to their immediate neighbours ('red' by its relationships to 'yellow', 'blue', 'green' 'purple', etc.). Long-range interactions are mediated by intermediaries, often resulting in metaphors. When the metaphor has become fixed, it means that the network has altered its structure to such an extent that the words have become neighbours (in the sense of network topology).

The reflexivity of language – the loops in the network – is exemplified by the dynamics of *différance*. Language is constantly transformed by the way in which it is used. The frequent use of a term, for example, can cause that term either to limit its semantic field (because we have grown too accustomed to it), or to expand it (because it is used inappropriately or in different contexts). The use of the term thus shifts the meaning of the term itself. As language is an open system, it interacts with the environment in many ways. New aspects of the environment will have effects on language. Words that have been used innocently for a long time (e.g. 'chairman') can suddenly become controversial. We are also forced, especially in the postmodern world, to come up with new words for new things all the time.

If language is closed off, if it is formalised into a stable system in which meaning is fixed, it will die, or was dead to start with. A living language is in a state far from equilibrium. It changes, it is in contact with other languages, it is abused and transformed. This does not mean that meaning is a random or arbitrary process. It means that meaning is a *local* phenomenon, valid in a certain frame of time and space. Since every language also has a history – a history co-responsible for the meaning of terms – meaning is more stable than one would think, even within the context of a model that values flux and proliferation. Words bear with them the traces of previous meanings that cannot be discarded at will. Above all, language is a system in which individual words do not have significance of their own. Meaning is only generated when individual words are caught in the play of the system.

The problems with a representational theory of meaning have been discussed in detail in Chapter 5, and I will not repeat the discussion here. The culmination of the argument there was the rejection of theories which separate the syntactic and semantic levels. The point was not only made from a post-structural perspective, but also incorporated arguments from Putnam's critique of classical representation. I do, however, want to return to the discussion of language as a self-organising system.

Those who support a post-structural understanding of language are often confronted with the following question: if language is constituted by a set of relationships among signifiers, how do you account for the relationship between language and the world? The concern here is that if meaning is ascribed to the play of signs only, language will become free-floating to the extent that no empirical truth claims can be made anymore. Although this objection is usually motivated by a nostalgia for a coherent metanarrative capable of regulating the production of meaning, it does pose a question that deserves a careful answer.

I have already argued that a pairing off of words and objects in a direct fashion – classical mimetic representation – is not acceptable. It does not give enough credit to the fact that language is a complex system. It assumes the existence of an objective, external viewpoint and begs the question as to the identity of the *agent* that performs this 'pairing off'. The relationship between language and the world is neither direct and transparent nor objectively controlled, but there *is* such a relationship – without it natural language would not exist. By understanding language as a self-organising system, we can start sketching a more sophisticated theory of this relationship.

Self-organisation describes how a complex system can develop and change its internal structure. The process is driven by competition for the resources of the system. Information from the environment enters the system (through some sensing mechanism) and interacts with information already encoded and stored in the system, causing the system to adapt and change its responses to the environment. All of this was described in Chapter 6. There we focused on the brain and neural networks as self-organising systems, but equivalent arguments would hold for language.

The important point for our discussion here is the fact that information from the environment has a direct, though non-determinate, influence on the system: it *causes* certain changes in the system, but it does not fully *determine* the nature of these changes. Information from the environment interacts in a non-linear way with information already stored in the system. (Bear in mind that the memory of the system is distributed, not iconic.) Incoming signals are mediated by the history of the system in such a way that it incorporates important new aspects, but resists unnecessary fluctuations. The state of the system at any given time is thus the result of conditions in the environment, the history of the system and the effects that the system must have on its environment in order to perform its functions.

How does language in fact interact with the environment (the 'world out there')? Primarily through the *users* of language who have to interact with the environment in order to survive and operate in it. As a matter of fact, language is one of the most important tools we use to cope with the task.

We try to make sense of our experiences, and in the process create and expand our language. This is not the result of an act by an abstract mind, nor a mere reflection of circumstances. Meaningful language evolves in time through a self-organising process, suspended between active and passive, in which useful or effective forms of language survive, and obsolete forms decay. An example may help to illustrate this. The word 'cow' (or some equivalent) can enter into someone's language through different mechanisms – including definition (indicating the relationships through the use of terms already known) and ostentation. However, none of these mechanisms are sufficient by themselves as a basis for an adequate theory of language. The word 'cow' will acquire meaning to the extent that cows are important to the user of language, and also, of course, to the extent it interacts with those elements that are already part of the user's linguistic system. The term is compared to other terms already available so as to satisfy present constraints. The term may originally be quite inaccurate (nothing more specific than 'fairly large, black and white animal'). The meaning of the term will develop proportional to the importance the term has. If, for example, you are a judge of cattle on important international shows for stud animals, the term 'cow' will be differentiated into a large number of finer details. If you are a city boy, the term may only have a few weak connotations with 'milk', 'steak', and a number of insults you do not really understand.

If language can be described as a self-organising system, the problem of the relationship between language and the world is solved in a fairly sophisticated way. The world has a direct causal influence on the meaning of words, but it does not *determine* the exact meaning of words. Meaning flows from a complex process of interaction between information from the world, on the one hand, and a web of already existing relationships, built up through previous interactions, on the other hand. This makes language a vital, evolving system, capable of coping with great complexity. If certain aspects of the environment are of great importance, the system will organise itself towards a robust, accurate interpretation of these aspects. It will not waste its resources by allocating too much of it to terms that are used infrequently or are of little interest. This kind of interpretation of language allows us to find an important place for the dynamics of trace and *différance*; it also leads us to acknowledge that the linguistic system will organise itself to a point of criticality where the maximum amount of meaning can be generated without becoming unanchored from the world.

The relationship between language and the world is always of interest, but all the more so when we do science. Then we have a responsibility to be as clear about this relationship as circumstances allow. Let us therefore examine the relationship between science and postmodern theory from the perspective of complex systems.

UNDERSTANDING SCIENTIFIC KNOWLEDGE FROM A POSTMODERN PERSPECTIVE

If we can describe language without invoking a meta-position, but rather in terms of a complex but robust system that helps us to cope with the world, we should be able to do something similar for the status of scientific knowledge. I will once again make use of Lyotard's analysis of the conditions of scientific knowledge in postmodern society, but the discussion will be introduced by a quote from Wilden (1987: 309).

> [The] revolt against simplicity made the neglected topic of complexity, or more accurately, *organised complexity* (constrained diversity), into a subject worthy of attention by scientists – biologists, ecologists, philosophers, humanists, culture critics, and others.
>
> This many-levelled revolution in favor of diversity is coming about at a time when we know for a fact that we may all end up nuked or puked.
>
> Our long-range future – if we have one – is now utterly dependent on those in power coming to understand the basic fact of the new science: that the open system that destroys its environment ultimately destroys itself.
>
> Organized complexity is the fount of life, liberty, and novelty on the planet earth.

In the first place, Wilden provides a definition of complexity that is consistent with the understanding of complexity developed in this study. He emphasises the principle of *organisation* in order to make sure that complexity is not confused with chaos. Complex systems are constrained, they have an organised structure, but within those constraints the system has to diversify maximally. The study of complexity, once neglected, can now be approached in a scientific way.

The second important point raised here by Wilden concerns the *nature* of this scientific approach. Instead of seeing science as an isolated element in a closed, fragmented social system, he stresses the political and social importance of the science of complexity.

We need to come to grips with complexity in order to ensure our survival. At the same time, complexity is the fount of liberty. In both science and politics, therefore, the acknowledgement of complexity is a vital step. Liberty and justice will not come about through the imposition of universal laws by some form of central control, nor will science flourish if it maintains a closed shop and speaks a private language. Scientific activities need to be more open, not only towards the world, but also internally. The barriers between the various scientific disciplines need to be crossed.

These points are explicitly confirmed by Lyotard, who also claims that scientific knowledge has traditionally been legitimated internally, i.e. the criteria by which something qualified as scientific were determined by science itself. Lyotard (1984: 25–26) notes the following five properties of this conservative approach, an approach to which he refers as the 'pragmatics of science':

(i)   Scientific knowledge requires that one language game – denotation – be retained and all others excluded. Although other types of statements, such as interrogatives or prescriptives, crop up in the process, they only present 'turning points in the dialectical argument which must end in a denotative statement' (25). A scientist is one who can produce such statements, verifiable or falsifiable, and intelligible only to the experts in the field.

(ii)   Scientific knowledge generated in this way is not part of the general 'social bond', but the property of the experts and professionals who organise themselves into exclusive institutes and institutions. 'The relation between knowledge and society . . . becomes one of mutual exteriority' (25).

(iii) In the process of research, only the competence of the researcher is at stake. Competence is not required from the receiver of the message or the subject of research (in the case of human sciences). 'A person does not have to know how to be what knowledge says he is' (26).

(iv)   Scientific statements do not increase their validity by being reported or through popularity. Any such statement is only as valid as its proof.

(v)   Scientific knowledge is cumulative. Scientists are supposed to know the accepted body of knowledge in their field and should only add new statements when they differ from previous ones.

This kind of knowledge – scientific knowledge – is contrasted with a more general kind of knowledge, what Lyotard calls 'narrative knowledge'. The pragmatics of narrative knowledge are also described in terms of a few properties (18–23):

(i)   The criteria for narrative knowledge are flexible and are dynamically defined by the society in which the narrative functions.

(ii)   No specific linguistic form is privileged in these narratives. They lend themselves to a variety of language games.

(iii) In the 'transmission' of these narratives, sender, receiver and the subjects discussed are all considered in a way that strengthens the social bond.

(iv)   Narratives have a strange temporal nature. Their function is not primarily to *remember* the past, but to re-enact past events as present events. The meaning of the narrative lies not in the fact that it is supported by some important piece of history, but in the metre and rhythm of its present telling.

(v)   No special procedure is necessary to 'authorise' the narrative process. The narrator is not isolated, but performs the function of integrator, and all those who participate can find themselves in any of the available roles (narrator, narratee, hero, etc.).

These two forms of knowledge – scientific and narrative – Lyotard claims, have been kept apart so long that they have become incommensurable. Narrative knowledge may include some aspect of scientific knowledge, but scientific knowledge is *legitimated* separately. Narrative statements cannot be the subject of argumentation and proof (27). The separation of the two has, however, led to a legitimation crisis for scientific knowledge in the postmodern era during which metanarratives are treated with incredulity. The decline of the scientific metanarrative is, however, not merely the result of some kind of theoretical approach, but a necessary result of the diversity and complexity that science has to deal with now.

> The 'crisis' of scientific knowledge, signs of which have been accumulating since the end of the nineteenth century, is not born of a chance proliferation of sciences, itself an effect of progress in technology and the expansion of capitalism. It represents, rather, an internal erosion of the legitimacy principle of knowledge. There is erosion at work inside the speculative game, and by loosening the weave of the encyclopedic net in which each science was to find its place, it eventually sets them free.
>
> (39)

This new freedom is important not only for the relationship between science and society, but also for the development of a new understanding of scientific knowledge and the practice of science itself. The traditional divisions among scientific disciplines no longer have a standing that cannot be challenged. As a matter of fact, contemporary science is at its most interesting where disciplines intersect: biotechnology, genetic computational algorithms, cyber-networks and virtual realities. 'The speculative hierarchy of learning gives way to an immanent and, as it were, "flat" network of areas of inquiry, the respective frontiers of which are in constant flux' (39).[4]

Lyotard here allocates two important characteristics to scientific inquiry. Firstly, it is immanent, i.e. contingent. This implies that, as in the case of narrative knowledge, its value is determined by participants of the game in terms of their present needs and constraints. Secondly, areas of inquiry are interconnected in a 'flat' network. We are already aware of the importance of understanding postmodern society as a network, but we must bear in mind that this network is 'flat'. It is not supported from below by some foundation, nor held together from above through general abstractions. We can only trace various narrative routes through a complex, flat network.

We now possess a framework for developing a 'narrative' interpretation of scientific knowledge. Instead of being denotative, external, self-centred, logical and historically cumulative, scientific knowledge is produced through interaction and diversity, and has become more and more embedded within the context of the wider social network. Science, as well, can only survive by entering the agonistics of the network.

The criteria for useful knowledge are no longer denotative, but more flexible. Because it forms part of an open system, it has to take the wider scenario into account. It cannot depend solely on the authority of either history,[5] or the expert, to legitimate it. Scientific knowledge, like the social network, organises itself in a manner that ensures only those narratives making a difference – in contingent, not abstract terms – will be perpetuated. There is no reason to fear, as some modernists do, that this would lead to less, or less reliable, knowledge than would following a conservative approach.

The idea of narrative knowledge that is also scientific can now be summarised. The world we live in is complex. This complexity is diverse but organised, not chaotic. Descriptions of it cannot be reduced to simple, coherent and universally valid discourses. If we model complexity in terms of a network, any given narrative will form a path, or trajectory, through the network. There are a great diversity of such paths. The network is not only complex, but also dynamic. As we trace various narrative paths through it, it changes. However, all paths are constrained by the local structure of the network. In some places these constraints can be fairly loose, in others they can be quite tight. The fact that there are many narrative paths to follow, even between two specific points, does not imply that anything goes. All narratives are subject to some form of constraint, and some paths are ruled out. All paths share the characteristics of contingency and provisionality. For strategic reasons, certain parts of the network can be closed off and fixed. This process of 'framing' is a necessary part of scientific inquiry, but the knowledge hereby produced remains relative to that specific frame and cannot be generalised in either a temporal or spatial sense.

At this point, a few other thinkers who have an understanding of science similar to the one derived from Lyotard, can be mentioned briefly. Blackwell (1976) suggests a framework for what he calls 'a structuralist account of scientific theories'. He does not mention any postmodern or post-structuralist authors, but acknowledges his indebtedness to Piaget (264). Nevertheless, his arguments have a familiar ring to them. He states that 'almost all theories of knowledge in Western philosophy are based on the notion that there are epistemological ultimates' (263). As examples he cites Plato's Forms, Aristotle's four causes, Descartes's innate ideas, Locke's primary qualities, Hume's simple impressions, Kant's forms of sensibility and categories of understanding, Peirce's ideal state of science, Husserl's essences, Russell's sense data and Carnap's logical atomistic building blocks of the world (263–264). Blackwell then denies the existence of epistemological ultimates and proposes a more modest outlook that admits 'that our personal experience as well as the accumulated evidence available to us is limited to a relatively short stretch of space and time' (264). In giving accounts of our knowledge, we always have to begin where we find ourselves: in mid-stream. It is in order to cope with this state of affairs that he proposes a 'structuralist' account.

Following Piaget, he defines a structure as 'any organised system of transformations which are governed by laws and which are self-regulatory' (266). He emphasises that a structure is 'a system of transformations, rather than a system of parts or elements' (267). The self-maintenance (read self-organisation) of the system is aimed at maintaining the dynamic structure and not the existence of any specific element (268). In developing scientific theories, one should not fall for the temptation of identifying basic elements and then ask how they are combined to form a theory. 'This is precisely the wrong approach and, in our opinion, is the main reason for the failure of contemporary philosophy of science to formulate an adequate account of theories' (269).

According to his 'mid-stream principle', theories have no ultimate elements, only intermediate ones. One should focus not on the elements, but on the system. Theories are hereby 'designated as processes, not as static, logical formalisms' (269). Although he does not refer to complexity or the need for diversity, Blackwell shows a sensitivity to the contingency of scientific knowledge as well as to the role of self-organisation – a process which allows for continuity in the structure of the system while it is adapting to new circumstances.

Mary Hesse is another thinker who is apprehensive about traditional analytical philosophy of science (Hesse 1992: 49). Her arguments are presented in the context of Anglo-American philosophy, and although they do not include elements of structuralist or postmodern thinking,[6] she has a keen interest in the complex nature of language and the ways in which it provides access to the world. She argues that metaphor is a 'fundamental form of language, and prior (historically and logically) to the literal' (54). An emphasis on metaphor and analogical reasoning shifts the focus of the philosophy of science from deductive reasoning to the problems of categorisation and clustering (Hesse 1988: 324). Using Wittgenstein's notion of family resemblances, she argues that we gain cognitive knowledge not by exhaustively calculating all the logical relations at stake in a particular instance, but rather by finding enough analogies to place this instance relative to others we are already happy with.

Clustering together things with related characteristics is of course exactly what a self-organising neural network does. Although Hesse does not explicitly use connectionist terms, she does work with the concept of a 'resemblance network' (324), and many of the points she makes are commensurable with a connectionist model of complexity. That much is clear from her advocacy of a moderate scientific realism, of knowledge that 'turns out to be particular rather than general, local rather than universal, approximate rather than exact, immediately describable and verifiable rather than theoretically deep and reductive' (Hesse 1992: 53).

Joseph Rouse is explicit in his adoption of postmodern elements in his development of a philosophy of science with a narrative structure. His central claim is formulated thus: 'the intelligibility, significance, and justification of scientific knowledge stem from their already belonging to continually reconstructed narrative contexts supplied by the ongoing social practices of scientific research' (Rouse 1990: 181). Unfortunately he does not concentrate on the development of such a 'narrative reconstruction of science'. Instead he attempts a kind of mapping of the territory of the philosophy of science to see who fits in where, with specific reference to the way in which the Modern discourse persists in the philosophy of science (Rouse 1991a). In this respect he makes the following remark:

> Thus I take the quintessentially modernist feature of much recent philosophy and sociology of science to be the posing of a stark alternative: *either* realism or rational methodology on the one hand, *or* relativism and the debunking of the alleged cultural hegemony of sciences on the other.
>
> (Rouse 1991b: 608)

From this position he concludes that radical post-positivist philosophers of science like Kuhn, Lakatos and Feyerabend are actually still part of modernity. He admits that this may sound odd at first, but, following Hacking, clarifies it by saying that we should think of 'modernity' not as a position, but as a 'shared field of conflict for which there must be a great deal of underlying agreement in order to make sharp and consequential disagreement possible' (610). A postmodern philosophy of science has to escape from the structure of this 'either/or', but Rouse does not really elaborate on how this should be done.

In a slightly earlier article, which makes no direct reference to postmodern thinkers, but recognises an indebtedness to Heidegger, Rouse (1990) does make his understanding of the generality of scientific knowledge clear. Here he is concerned with the thorny issue of the *coherence* of the scientific narrative. On the one hand, Rouse rejects the idea of the unity of science 'which postulates as an epistemic ideal the unification of scientific representations of the world into a single all-inclusive and coherent picture' (192). He motivates this rejection by denying that the goal of science is the 'accumulation of a body of representations abstracted from the activity of research' (192). The advance of science is centrifugal rather than centripetal, and in this process established results are often left by the wayside. The concerns of science are practical rather than representational, and insofar as there is a concern for coherence, it is only local, more local even than the level of the applicable discipline, let alone that of the whole of science.

On the other hand, Rouse claims that there is a different and important sense in which scientific knowledge does get unified. This has to do with the fact that the boundaries between disciplines are regularly breached, not only by scientists plundering other disciplines for tools and ideas, but also by the hybrid disciplines that are developing as increasingly complex issues are addressed.

What we get is not a single coherent picture of the world, but an ever more complex network of interconnections binding together various scientific endeavours. . . . [T]he loss in coherence is often happily compensated by the creation of new possibilities to explore, and new capabilities for doing that.

(192–193)

His sensitivity for the importance of competition is also worth mentioning: 'To be "technical" simply *is* to be a response to a history of conflicts' (188). Given this framework, we can conclude that although Rouse does not elaborate on the actual dynamics of scientific knowledge in postmodern society, he should not object to the 'agonistics of the network' suggested by my reading of Lyotard.

In his latest book, however, Rouse (1996) does little more than pay lip service to the idea of postmodern science. Apart from some references to gender issues, the ethical dimension of scientific practice is not explored and there is no engagement with continental theory. Thinkers like Lyotard and Derrida are mentioned only *en passant*. For me, reading this book was about as pleasant as it would be to eat it.

The next theorist I wish to discuss turns out to be a disappointment as well, at least within the context of the approach taken in this study. Paul Churchland is a strong advocate of the importance of the neurocomputational approach. He and Patricia Churchland were some of the first philosophers to explore the philosophical implications of neural networks (P.M. Churchland 1984, 1989; P.M. Churchland and P.S. Churchland 1990; P.S.Churchland 1986; P.S. Churchland and Sejnowski 1992). The issue at stake is not whether they accept and employ connectionist models, but *how* they do it. This issue can be tackled by looking at *A Neurocomputational Perspective* in which Paul Churchland (1989) examines the importance of neural networks for the theory of scientific knowledge.

In an essay entitled 'The Ontological Status of Observables: In Praise of Superempirical Virtues' (139–151) he positions himself as a realist asserting 'that global excellence of theory is the ultimate measure of truth and ontology at all levels of cognition, even at the observational level' (139). His realism is more circumspect than may be deduced from this passage (141), but he remains committed to the idea that there is a world that exists independent of our 'cognition', and that we construct *representations* of this world (151). Since different representations are possible, they have to be compared, and the best selected. The selection cannot be made on the basis of 'empirical facts', but 'must be made on superempirical grounds such as relative coherence, simplicity, and explanatory unity' (146). It should be clear that from this position he is not about to explore contingency, complexity and diversity.

Churchland's approach is not naïve or unsophisticated, as can be seen from the central essay, 'On the Nature of Theories' (153–196). According to

him, the classical view of a theory is that it is 'a set of sentences or proposi-
tions, expressible in the first order predicate calculus' (153). In that view,
theories are *statable*. Only theories of this kind can perform the primary
functions of theories, i.e. prediction, explanation and intertheoretical reduction; they promise an account of the nature of learning and of rationality
(in formal terms), and their ultimate virtue is truth (153). Churchland rejects
the view that sentential and propositional attitudes are 'the most important
form of representation used by cognitive creatures' (158), and suggests that
one should rather look at the way in which the brain 'represents and
computes' (159). After an introduction to neural networks (or parallel
distributed processing) he discusses the implications the latter have for the
nature of theories. One important aspect that he does point out is the
following: an explanation of what a neural network does can only be given
at the level of the weights (177). The need for higher level (logical) explanations is therefore eliminated.[7] Everything necessary to explain the behaviour
of the network is contained in the (material) values of the weights.

Although this point does concur with the position proposed in the
present study, Churchland understands it in a very *static* way. An explanation is provided by the collective values of the weights at a specific moment,
'a point in weight space' (177). Given his representational bent, this is
perhaps not surprising, but it does undermine an interpretation of explanation and understanding as *processes*. This may be in part because
Churchland uses, as I do, the simple, one-directional 'back-propagation'
network to explain the working of a neural network. Although he recognises
the importance of recurrent networks (208), he does not expand on the
dynamics of these networks. I could therefore find no analyses of the process
of self-organisation – a process for which recurrency is a prerequisite.

Another important conclusion he draws from the model of the network is
that all empirical observations are theory-laden. Since information entering
the network can only be processed in terms of the patterns of weights
already existing, 'no cognitive activity whatsoever takes place in the absence
of some theory or other' (188). Such a viewpoint is closer to the one taken in
this study, but he still refers to the goal of theory formation as the development of partitions of the weight space into 'useful and well-structured
subdivisions' (189).[8] There is nothing *a priori* about these divisions since
Churchland is willing to discard the notion of truth 'in pursuit of some epistemic goal even *more* worthy than truth' (150). What this goal might be,
however, is not mentioned.

In summary, Churchland's employment of neural networks as explanatory tool is an important step, but to my mind it is seriously hampered by
his continued commitment to the importance of representation. He does not
believe in the existence of a single, correct representation, and consequently
he sees no hope for convergent realism (194), which must bring him quite
close to discarding the notion of representation. However, he clings to the
idea that the world has to be 'carved up', and that networks perform the

carving by developing representations. His final article of faith remains the following:

> Our best and most penetrating grasp of the real is still held to reside in the representations provided by our best theories. Global excellence of theory remains the fundamental measure of rational ontology. And that has always been the central claim of scientific realism.
>
> (151)

Finally I want to mention a book that constitutes a project that is not all that different to mine, but arrives at opposite conclusions. In *A Blessed Rage for Order: Deconstruction, Evolution, and Chaos*, Alexander J. Argyros (1991) examines the work of Derrida, and then discards it. His approach is a conservative one, and by his own admission, 'a kind of foundationalism' (2). He is firmly committed to the ideal of progress (323–331), at times with a zeal that sounds pious: 'If we are to replace the emperor [the naked one – that favourite metaphor of modern conservatives] with something better, we must believe, and deeply, that better alternatives are possible' (5). Given this approach, it comes as no surprise that he focuses on chaos theory as the kind of science that should lead us to the promised land: '[Chaos theory] can serve to begin healing the four-hundred-year-old schism between science and the humanities. In addition, chaos may allow us to reaffirm such battered concepts as universality, identity, meaning, truth, and beauty' (7).

The basic premise of Argyros's book is not really at odds with my argument. He claims that the natural world, as revealed by natural science, of course, 'channels human interpretations of both culture and nature as much as human interpretations of culture and nature are channeled by sociohistorical pressures' (2). Despite the fact that this claim seems to have a circular component – human interpretation is guided by the world *as revealed by science*, which itself of course involves interpretation – my quarrel is not with the claim, but with Argyros's conclusion that Derrida would contest such a position.

His understanding of post-structuralism is clearly influenced by a strain of American literary theory that likes to see post-structuralism as something anarchistic and destructive. It is this severely limited understanding of Derrida that leads him to claim that 'deconstruction, and all antifoundationalisms, must bracket the entirety of the natural world, including that part of it comprising the non-mindlike components of human beings' (2), and that 'for deconstructionists, any dialogue with nature can only be a disguised monologue' (3). From this it is clear that for Argyros, post-structuralism is an idealism that denies any importance to the human body and to the world as it is. It is exactly this kind of understanding of post-structural theory that I contest, and, I am convinced, so would Derrida. It is also a pity that Argyros chooses what is generally considered to be one of Derrida's weaker pieces – his essay on apartheid[9] – for detailed analysis.

Let me repeat the position stated in Chapter 1: there is no *imperative* to subscribe to the post-structural position when we deal with complex, dynamic systems. I find it extremely helpful, and therefore important, but it is possible to make points similar to mine from other perspectives. In the case of Argyros, however, I feel that his basic conservatism has forced him to turn a potential ally into a foe.

In this section I have explored the nature of scientific knowledge in the context of connectionist models. My central point has been that our descriptions of the world need to have an inherent sensitivity for complexity. Through the examination of a number of theoretical frameworks, it has become clear that postmodern and post-structural theories do have such a sensitivity, and, furthermore, that a reading of these theories from a connectionist perspective suggests that the notions of patterns and constraints are inherent to post-structuralism. The existence of contingent constraints argues against an interpretation of these theories as implying that 'anything goes'. I have also shown that the acceptance of connectionist models does not by itself lead to a deeper understanding of complexity. That is why I would insist on the fruitfulness of combining complexity theory with post-structuralism.

THE COMPLEXITY OF POSTMODERN ETHICS

I wish to return to Lyotard's (1984) claims that his analysis of the post-modern condition provides us with 'the outline of a politics that would respect both the desire for justice and the desire for the unknown' (67). Here Lyotard flies in the face of those who feel that the absence of all meta-descriptions (or prescriptions) makes the postmodern condition fundamentally unethical. Their objection is that any form of critique that is not backed up by objective criteria, or at least by some form of consensus, can be dismissed too easily. Lyotard singles out Habermas as one who would adopt this kind of approach, but argues that such an approach is 'neither possible, nor even prudent' (45).

Lyotard claims that Habermas's approach, consisting of what he calls a 'dialogue of argumentation', rests on two assumptions: in the first place, it assumes that 'it is possible for all speakers to come to agreement on which rule or metaprescriptions are universally valid for all language games'; and in the second place, it assumes 'that the goal of dialogue is consensus' (65). Lyotard finds neither of these assumptions acceptable, primarily because they deny the complexity of postmodern society – the nature of which he describes in the following way:

> It is a monster formed by the interweaving of various networks of hetero-morphous classes of utterances (denotative, prescriptive, performative, technical, evaluative, etc.). There is no reason to think that it could be possible to determine metaprescriptives common to all of these language games or that a revisable consensus like the one in force at a given

moment in the scientific community could embrace the totality of metaprescriptions regulating the totality of statements circulating in the social collectivity. As a matter of fact, the contemporary decline of narratives of legitimation – be they traditional or 'modern' (the emancipation of humanity, the realization of the Idea) – is tied to the abandonment of this belief.

(65)

The first assumption of the Habermasian approach is directly opposed to Lyotard's emphasis on the proliferation of heterogeneous discourses and the role of paralogy, while the second is opposed to his insistence on the importance of dissent. Not that consensus is *always* impossible; it can be achieved, but only as a local phenomenon limited in both time and space. Consensus as a goal would attempt to freeze the social system into a particular state. Since it is unlikely that this will be achieved (as well as undesirable), a better (and more just) policy would be to develop a sensitivity for the *process* of social transformation. This may indicate that 'consensus has become an outmoded and suspect value', but, claims Lyotard, 'justice as a value is neither outmoded nor suspect' (66).

Given the complexity of postmodern society, the concept of justice is certainly a problematic one, but Lyotard recognises two important, if predictable, strategies: the recognition of the heteromorphous nature of language games; and the recognition of the fact that all agreements on the rules of any discourse, as well as on the 'moves' allowed within that discourse, *must* be local, in other words, 'agreed on by its present players and subject to eventual cancellation' (66).

This proposal sketches the outline for a practical theory of justice that can best be understood as follows. It becomes the responsibility of every player in any discursive practice to know the rules of the language game involved. These rules are local, i.e. 'limited in time and space' (66). In following such rules, one has to assume responsibility both for the rules themselves and for the effects of that specific practice. This responsibility cannot be shifted to any universally guiding principles or institutions – whether they be the State, the Church or the Club.

The question that should be posed at this point is the following: can behaviour in accordance with an abstract, universal set of rules be called 'ethical' at all? What is at stake here is the very meaning of the word 'ethics'. It was part of the dream of modernism to establish a universal set of rules that would be able to regulate our behaviour in every circumstance. Taken by itself, this is a noble ideal, but if we wish to argue that human beings are *constituted* by their ethical behaviour, we run into problems. Following a universal set of rules (assuming such rules exist) does not involve decision or dilemma, it merely asks for calculation. Given the circumstances, what do the rules decree my behaviour should be? Can this be called 'ethical'? What kind of human being would act like this? Clearly some kind of automaton, itself constituted by rational, rule-based principles. Modernist ethics, and an understanding of language and the mind in terms of rule-based systems, fit together perfectly.

This concurs with Zygmunt Bauman's (1992, 1993) analysis of modern and postmodern ethics. For him, modernism's attempt to structure our existence leads to nothing less than our imprisonment. A postmodern attitude sets us free, not to do as we like, but to behave ethically. He acknowledges that this involves a paradox: 'it restores to agents the fullness of moral choice and responsibility while simultaneously depriving them of the comfort of the universal guidance that that modern self-confidence once promised. . . . Moral responsibility comes with the loneliness of moral choice' (Bauman 1992: xxii). Actually this is just another formulation of the principle that has become a *leitmotiv* of this chapter: you cannot escape the agonistics of the network.

How does this principle influence moral behaviour in practice, and does it really mean that all ethical principles are so contingent as to be ephemeral? Difficult questions of this kind are addressed in the work of Druscilla Cornell (1992). Her aim is to 'establish the relationship of the philosophy of the limit [the term she employs to describe her interpretation of post-structural theory] to the questions of ethics, justice, and legal interpretation' (1). She concentrates on the work of Adorno, Derrida and Levinas, and although she is mainly concerned with the field of jurisprudence, I am of the opinion that most of the arguments presented in this book will support her position.

Cornell certainly supports the notion that we are all constituted by a complex set of relationships, and she analyses different interpretations of this position, taking Hegel as an important point of reference. In his criticism of Kant's abstract idealism, Hegel realises that we are constituted within the social system, but for him it is a system that will ultimately be perfectly organised. Everybody will have their specified place. Although Hegel realised that the (dialectical) process of organisation is still in progress, his view is, in the end, still a conservative one. At some stage there will be no further need for transformation. Adorno argues that there are differences among human beings that remain irreducible to a totalising system. He thus reminds us of the importance of differences, not as something that prevents us from finding a comfortable place in the system, but as that which constitutes our humanity.

As an example of a contemporary thinker who analyses the implications of a system's theory for ethical issues, Cornell (116–154) discusses the work of Niklas Luhmann. Luhmann sees society as a complex, self-organising system. Since we are part of this system – we can actually never stand outside it – we have no choice but to accept that the system will organise itself in the way best for its survival. The system will 'evolve', but cannot be 'transformed'. We have no choice but to stay 'inside' the system. The present understanding of, for example, a legal principle is therefore the correct one –

a conservative, even positivistic, conclusion. This is a 'weak' kind of post-modernism, an example of the kind of constructivism that Argyros (see above) objects to. It may come as some surprise to him that it is Derrida whom Cornell uses to counter Luhmann's understanding of society as a self-contained, complete system.

The crux of the Cornell/Derrida argument is their interpretation of the flow of time in a system (128). Traditional interpretations of the temporal nature of a system, including Luhmann's position, privilege the present. The immense gain of the notion of *différance* is that it reminds us that not only the past has to be considered when we try to establish the meaning of (say) an event, but that since we cannot fully predict the effects of this event, the future has to be considered as well, despite the fact that we have no idea what this future might be. Now, instead of throwing up his hands, and declaring that in such a case it is impossible to talk about meaning, and that therefore anything goes, Derrida insists that we should take responsibility for this unknowable future. In the case of ethical decisions, this leads to an aporia (133–135): we have to take responsibility for the future effects of our decisions, but we cannot know those effects, nor can we wait to see what they are. We have to make the decision now.

How do we deal with this aporia? To fall back on universal principles is to deny the complexity of the social system we live in, and can therefore never be just. To allow everything is to evade our responsibility. The first approach to the system is too rigid, the second too fluid. Cornell's suggestion (following Derrida, and reformulated in my terminology) is to take present ethical (and legal) principles seriously – to resist change – but to be keenly aware of when they should not be applied, or have to be discarded. We therefore do follow principles *as if they were universal rules* (Cornell and Derrida use the term 'quasi-transcendental'), but we have to remotivate the legitimacy of the rule *each time we use it*. To behave ethically means not to follow rules blindly – to merely calculate – but to follow them responsibly, which may imply that the rules must be broken. It is important to emphasise that in these circumstances breaking a rule does not invalidate it. That would have been the case if the rule were part of an abstract set of rules bound by logical relationships. But if it is a quasi-rule emerging from a complex set of relationships, part of the *structure* of this kind of rule will be the possibility *not* to follow it. To make a responsible judgement – whether it be in law, science or art – would therefore involve at least the following components:

- Respecting otherness and difference as values in themselves.
- Gathering as much information on the issue as possible, notwithstanding the fact that it is impossible to gather *all* the information.
- Considering as many of the possible consequences of the judgement, notwithstanding the fact that it is impossible to consider *all* the consequences.
- Making sure that it is possible to revise the judgement as soon as it

becomes clear that it has flaws, whether it be under specific circumstances, or in general.

Admittedly, this brief discussion of Cornell's work does not do justice to the many issues she raises. The problems of ethics, justice and law – at a personal, national and international level – remain some of the most challenging, and most important to be faced. I hope to have shown that complexity theory, interpreted from a post-structural perspective, can help us to approach these issues better equipped.

8 Afterword: Understanding complexity

The aim of this book has been to stimulate transdisciplinary discussion on the subject of complexity. It is my contention that the traditional methods of science and analytical philosophy are not sensitive enough to the dynamics of complex systems. I have therefore been critical of the analytical method (carving things up), deductive logic, atomism, formal rule-based grammars, closed algorithms and symbolic representation. The shortcomings of these approaches have been pointed out in analyses of information theory, formal symbol systems, Searle's Chinese Room argument and Fodor's mental representationalism. As an alternative, I have proposed a connectionist approach, arguing that this approach is intrinsically more sensitive to complexity. It focuses on the behaviour of collections of many interconnected, similar elements that do not have (atomistic) significance by themselves, but that obtain significance through a complex set of non-linear, asymmetrical relationships in a network. Important characteristics of these networks include distributedness, self-organisation and the operation on local information without central control. I have also shown that these models already have practical applications, e.g. in pattern recognition problems, and that an understanding of them as complex systems can help to improve their practical performance. Throughout I have tried to intertwine philosophical and scientific discourses. The idea has been to show not only how philosophical considerations can benefit scientific practice, but also the reverse. It was specifically the burden of the final chapter to show how a practical understanding of complexity can contribute to some of the key areas in postmodern philosophy.

As far as the application of these models of complexity is concerned, this conclusion marks only the beginning. It must be clearly understood that the general understanding of complexity developed here does *not* supply a complete description of any *specific* complex system. If we want to analyse, for example, a living cell as a complex system, the ideas presented here merely provide a framework. The framework will have to be filled in with the (biochemical) detail relevant to the specific case. Similarly, we have characterised language in terms of a complex system, but this has to be seen as a very tentative first step. For the development of useful, wide-ranging

connectionist models of language, and for their implementation in machines
– should that prove to be possible – a great deal of very hard work still lies
ahead. My hope is that this study could provide a certain theoretical orienta-
tion when difficult and complex projects such as these are attempted.

Finally, I am very much aware of the fact that I could be criticised for
committing the performative fallacy, i.e. attempting to do what I claim is not
possible. In this case the problem would lie in trying to develop a theory that
insists on radical contingency, yet claims to be generally valid. This is exactly
the same problem that Derrida (1981: 26) faces when he claims 'there are only,
everywhere, differences and traces of traces'. To insist that this fallacy should
not be committed makes it extremely difficult to maintain any radically critical position. This demand marks the starkest division between the analytical
and the postmodern positions. What is seen as the ultimate knock-down argument on the one side is seen as an evasion of the real issues by the other.

Perhaps a truly postmodern response to this demand would be to just
ignore it. However, Derrida responded quite strongly when this kind of
accusation was made against him by Habermas,[1] and perhaps I should take
the risk of responding as well. I cannot counter the argument on its own
grounds – in that respect it is a show stopper. However, I do think that one
should consider the *contents* of the theory being accused of the performative
fallacy. Just like Derrida's theory of the trace, the characterisation of
complexity presented here is a very sparse one; it claims very little. It
describes in general the structure of complex systems, but at a very low level.
This means that the higher-level or emergent properties play no role as such
in the theory itself; they have no 'higher' importance. Just as Derrida's
model of language is held together by traces only, complex systems are held
together by local interactions only. The model does not attempt to specify
the effects of those interactions.

This argument can be explicated by referring, for the last time now, to a
similar problem concerning the training of neural networks. Neural
networks are said to be non-algorithmic in the way they solve problems, yet
the network is trained with a learning 'algorithm'. This learning algorithm,
however, knows absolutely nothing about the structure of the specific
problem being addressed. The same 'algorithm' can be used to change the
weights in networks that are applied to any number of problems. It operates
at such a low level that it has no content by itself, and is only given content
in specific, contingent applications. Similarly, the description of complexity
provided here does pretend to be general, but at a low level. It does not
pretend to provide an accurate, detailed description of any specific complex
system. As a matter of fact, it remains sceptical of such descriptions exactly
because of the dynamics apparent at the low level.

This point will surely not eliminate the charge of performing the performative fallacy, or other criticisms, for that matter, but hopefully it
communicates something of the spirit in which this book is offered: one of
openness, provisionality and adventure.

Notes

1 APPROACHING COMPLEXITY

1 These characteristics are adapted from similar descriptions in Nicolis and Prigogine (1989), Serra and Zanarini (1990) and Jen (1990).

2 The concept 'emergence' is often used in a way that creates the impression that something mysterious happens when 'things come together'. The way in which it is used here implies nothing ineffable whatsoever. It merely underlines the fact that nothing 'extra', no external telos or designer, is required to 'cause' the complex behaviour of a system. Perhaps it would be better to employ the term 'relational properties' rather than 'emergent properties'.

3 The example is chosen for didactic reasons. I have no detailed knowledge of economics.

4 In a certain sense, the economic system 'bottoms out' at the level of the penny. There is nothing below, nor is there anything above, this level. The economy is constituted by the movement of clusters of pennies. In Derrida's terms (to be discussed later), the penny is the 'trace' of the economic system.

5 For a detailed discussion of the development and significance of thermodynamics, and of the ways in which it opened up new avenues for research, see Prigogine and Stengers (1984).

6 Talking only about series of numbers may seem a little superficial, but bear in mind that any formalism can be expressed as a series of numbers via the Gödel numbering system.

7 To prove that a sequence is *not* random is easy, one only has to find a program that is shorter. It need not even be a minimal program. To prove that a sequence *is* random, however, you have to prove that no shorter program exists. Chaitin argues, following Gödel's Incompleteness Theorem, that such a proof cannot be found. Randomness is falsifiable, but never verifiable (this is a much stronger claim in mathematics than in the empirical sciences). Chaitin's conclusion concerning the implications of this argument for the limitations of number formalism is both interesting and important, but falls outside the scope of this study. For further details see Chaitin (1975: 50–53; 1987: 146–164).

8 The status of *all* states of a system cannot be determined from within the system. The 'incompleteness' of a formal system, in other terms also known as the 'halting problem', is a complex meta-mathematical issue analysed by Gödel (1962) and Turing (1936) respectively, and falls outside the scope of this study. For accessible discussions of these issues, see Hofstadter (1980) or Penrose (1989).

9 Whether a natural language can actually be modelled by a formal system is one of the great unresolved problems of modern linguistics. I will argue that rule-

based systems are *not* adequate models for the complexity of natural language. The example of a formal language given here is from within the AI perspective.

10 This is of course an oversimplification of the actual working of the brain, but even in such a reduced model we already have the capability for complex behaviour.

11 Their critique is discussed in Chapter 2.

12 They are adapted from discussions in Serra and Zanarini (1990: 26, 27) and Chandrasekaran *et al.* (1988).

13 In first-order logic, *anything* can be proven from contradictory premises. As soon as a contradiction occurs, the results of the logical deduction become meaningless.

2 INTRODUCING CONNECTIONISM

1 An equation for the output of a specific neuron can be given:

$$\varnothing = f\left(\sum_{l}^{n} O_n W_n\right)$$

with:

$\varnothing$ the output of this neuron

n the amount of preceding neurons connected to this one

O_n the output of the nth previous neuron

W_n the weight associated with the nth previous neuron

f the transfer function of the neuron, almost always a non-linear function, usually sigmoidal in shape

For a detailed, technical introduction to neural networks, see Rumelhart and McClelland (1986).

2 The concept of Turing machines can be misleading. They are abstract mathematical entities that provide formalisations with which to describe computational procedures, i.e. processes that follow an algorithm in discrete steps, including those implemented on digital computers with a Van Neumann architecture. The fact that Turing describes these 'machines' in terms of a 'tape head' that reads and prints symbols on a (sometimes infinitely long) 'tape' does not make them 'real'. For a more detailed discussion of Turing machines and their relationships to computers see Haugeland (1985: 133–140) or Penrose (1989: 40–86).

3 Their failure to distinguish between a semantic net and a distributed representation in a neural net also results in their equating of connectionism with associationism (Fodor and Pylyshyn 1988: 31). A connectionist network does not encode a number of relationships between specific ideas, because specific nodes in the network do not correspond to specific ideas, as they do in a semantic network. Some of this confusion is a result of connectionist terminology. Connectionists tend to refer to the relationships in a network as 'sub-symbolic' or as 'micro-features', as if a group of micro-features lumped together will add up to one whole feature or symbol. A better understanding of what a weight is emerges when it is compared with Derrida's notion of a 'trace' (see below).

4 Such research has received serious attention among connectionists long before Fodor *et al.* suggested it. See, e.g., Touretzky and Hinton (1985).

5 A similar argument can be used to defend a 'postmodern' form of rationality that is not based on universal principles, but emerges from the necessity to cope with – and be critical of – our complex life-world. Rationality cannot precede the generation of meaning, but must follow it; and meaning is the result of a complex set of relationships. See Schrag (1992) for a similar kind of argument, made from a philosophical – not connectionist – perspective.

6 This division between knowledge and ethics will be discussed in the final chapter.

3 POST-STRUCTURALISM, CONNECTIONISM AND COMPLEXITY

1 Throughout this introduction the concept 'sign' can be regarded as functionally equivalent to the connectionist notion of 'unit' or 'node' in a network.

2 Culler (1983: 96) provides the following example:

> If a cave man is successfully to inaugurate language by making a special grunt signify 'food', we must suppose that the grunt is already distinguished from other grunts and that the world has already been divided into the categories 'food' and 'non-food'.

3 For his own succinct summary of the notion of *différance*, see Derrida (1982: 89).

4 For a more detailed comparison, see Cilliers (1990).

4 JOHN SEARLE BEFUDDLES

1 Searle's argument leads Roger Schank to conclude that the only understanding that can be found is situated in the person writing the program, the AI researcher (Searle 1980: 447).

2 For a more detailed discussion see Marletti (1990).

3 The question concerning who are and who are not dualists could form a separate line of inquiry. Hofstadter (in Searle 1980: 433) is quite clear about his evaluation of Searle's status in this respect. He claims that Intentionality is merely Searle's word for 'soul'.

4 This essay, along with Derrida's response to Searle's critique and an extended Afterword, was anthologised under the title *Limited Inc.* (Derrida 1988). My references will be to the anthologised versions.

5 After having written this chapter, I encountered an article by Globus (1991) which also raises a number of objections, some of them similar to mine.

5 PROBLEMS WITH REPRESENTATION

1 Productivity and structure are also the two horns of the argument Fodor and Pylyshyn (1988) advance against connectionism. This was discussed in Chapter 2.

2 The transfer function of specific neurons can vary as well. This is of practical importance in finding economic implementation, but in theory the change in transfer function can be achieved by the addition of bias terms or, if necessary, by using a few extra neurons with transfer functions similar to the rest.

3 Of course, if the network has self-organising capabilities, the functions of lost

neurons can be taken over by others without having to build up a new representation from scratch. Self-organisation is discussed in the next chapter.

4 Sterelny (1990: 187) lists six 'serious problems'. Some of them are similar enough to be combined. I will also discuss them in a sequence different from the one in which he presented them.

5 Strictly speaking we should no longer use the word 'representation' in this context. Instead of introducing new and perhaps confusing terminology, I will continue to use the term, bearing in mind that the term 'distributed representation' contains internal contradictions. In the tradition of Heidegger one should perhaps have used 'distributed ~~representation~~'.

6 An expert system is a formal model of a domain of knowledge implemented on a computer by using sets of rules.

7 A classic example is the so-called exclusive–or (XOR) problem. It is used as a traditional test-case for classifiers since it constitutes a problem that is not linearly separable. Neural networks consisting of half a dozen neurons can solve the problem. I do not think that the analysis of such networks contributes much to our understanding of neurocomputing.

8 These parameters apply to the XOR problem. See note 7 above.

9 For example, at ICANN–92 – a large neural network conference (see Aleksander and Taylor 1992) – several papers addressed this issue. Judd (1992) showed that wide, shallow networks are computationally efficient, and Hecht-Nielsen (1992) argued that the high-dimensional networks necessary to solve complex problems have less difficulty converging than one may think.

10 The philosophical arguments provided here are certainly not the only ones against representation. Problems with representation is, for example, one of the central themes of Rorty's (1980) *Philosophy and the Mirror of Nature* – where he also engages with Chomsky and Fodor (244–256). Joseph Rouse (1996: 205–236) argues against representation from a Davidsonian perspective. Norris (1992: 59–82) analyses attempts to show similarities between Davidson and Derrida, and concludes that this comparison is not a simple one to make.

11 This issue is discussed at greater length, incorporating insights from both Wittgenstein and Derrida, by Schalkwyk (1991). The structural necessity for the sign to be iterable is one of the central issues at stake in the confrontation between Searle and Derrida (1988).

12 One could perhaps argue that both Baudrillard and Derrida want to collapse the Tower Bridge picture of representation, but not in the same way. Baudrillard, the more 'postmodern' of the two, collapses the picture to the top level – everything is simulation – whereas Derrida wants to collapse it to the bottom level – everything is material. If one falls for the idea of one level only, perhaps the difference does not matter so much. One can, however, see how Baudrillard's approach leads to the 'anything goes' style of postmodernism; something that is foreign to Derrida's understanding of the status of texts.

6 SELF-ORGANISATION IN COMPLEX SYSTEMS

1 There is an interesting tension between the need for structure and the need for plasticity. Some form of structure is a prerequisite for the encoding of information in the system, but if the structure is too rigid, it cannot adapt. Similarly, plasticity is necessary for adaptation, but if change can take place too easily – if the memory of the system is too short – the system merely reflects the surroundings, and cannot interpret it. This matter will receive more attention below.

2 Other models are provided by cellular automata (Serra and Zanarini 1990:

50–60; Toffoli and Margolus 1987) as well as *digital* cellular automata, also known as Random Boolean nets (Serra and Zanarini 1990: 64–69; Staufer 1987). Boolean nets are also used by Stuart Kauffman in his simulations of self-organising systems. Although Kauffman undoubtedly does important work, I will not discuss it. Part of the problem is that it is difficult to find a Kauffman text with which one can engage at a philosophical level. It would be helpful if he wrote a book finding a balance between the strict mathematics of *The Origins of Order* (Kauffman 1993) and the flowery, quasi-religious rhetoric of *At Home in the Universe* (Kauffman 1995).

3　In the case of the brain (which is a neural network), stimuli are received not only from the outside via the senses, but also from the inside of the body.

4　These principles are based on a similar list provided by Von der Malzburg (1987: 272).

5　Predefined structure is not excluded. In living systems important structures can be inherited.

6　Instances of entrainment found in nature include the following: populations of crickets entrain each other to chirp coherently; populations of fireflies move towards coherent flashing; and the ovulation cycles of women living closely together move in phase (Garfinkel 1987: 200).

7　The best example of a meta-stable state is that of an upside-down pendulum. The smallest perturbation will immediately push it out of the balanced state.

8　Ideally we need a formulation of the principle of selection that would be compatible with Hebb's rule (or the use-principle).

9　See Edelman (1987: 234, 235) for a discussion on the differences between the theory of direct perception (Gibson 1979) and neuronal group selection.

10　For an important discussion of the role of memory that incorporates the views of Freud and Edelman, see Rosenfeld (1988). Rosenfeld argues for a non-symbolic, non-representational theory of memory.

11　I owe this insight to Andries Gouws.

12　See Cornell (1992: 116–154) for a discussion of how the dynamics of *différance* deconstructs a linear understanding of time in the context of complex systems – in Cornell's case, the legal system.

7　COMPLEXITY AND POSTMODERNISM

1　In the previous chapter we encountered the notion of 'population thinking'. As a kind of equivalent – in the context of Lyotard's arguments in favour of a sensitivity to difference – we can coin the term 'difference thinking', alluding to the way in which members of a population can only be told apart on the basis of their differences from each other.

　　The choice of the word 'paralogy' is also significant. It is usually employed to designate *false* reasoning, to mark something as unlogical. The word literally means 'beside' logic, and Lyotard employs it to show that logical descriptions are not adequate when dealing with the richness and contradictions of contingent complexity. Many stories, even contradictory ones, can be told about single events or phenomena. Lyotard (1984: 60) distinguishes paralogy from 'innovation', which, he claims, is still under the command of the system, as it is used to improve the latter's efficiency. Paralogy is 'a move played in the pragmatics of knowledge', the consequences of which cannot be determined *a priori*.

2　Here Lyotard explicitly refers to Jean Baudrillard, whose analyses of postmodern society often have a very negative flavour.

3　In her analysis of social (or ethical) relationships, Druscilla Cornell (1992) is aware of the necessity of asymmetrical relationships as well. In order to minimise the possibilities of exploitation, she insists (following Derrida's reading of Levinas) on 'phenomenological symmetry' (85). The argument is that no element in the system is privileged in an *a priori* way. In their existence, all elements are equal. This is an important point to make, and does not conflict with our understanding of the elements in a complex system. It does not, however, supply any guarantee against exploitation, nor does it really help us to identify exploitation when we encounter it. The problem is that, to a large extent, the node in the network (and therefore the individual in the social system) is *constituted* by its relationships, not by some phenomenological aspect of the node itself. We have to grant the phenomenological equality of each individual, but, in all but the most obvious cases, to establish whether someone is being violated, we have to start disentangling the web of social relationships. These relationships are contingent, and therefore different each time.

4 It must be noted that Lyotard is somewhat ambiguous in his evaluation of this point. Although he shows that the 'potential for erosion' is intrinsic to traditional scientific discourse, it does seem as if he feels something important is lost in the process, some special kind of 'speculative' research that is only possible under the auspices of the 'faculty' associated with the traditional university (Lyotard 1984: 39, 52).

5 This point forms the basis of Lyotard's rejection of hermeneutics. Hermeneutic discourse is born of the presupposition that 'true knowledge . . . is composed of reported statements that are incorporated into the metanarrative of a subject that guarantees their legitimacy'. This is a presupposition 'which guarantees that there is meaning to know and thus confers legitimacy upon history (and especially the history of learning)' (Lyotard 1984: 35).

6 Rouse (1991b: 609) does, however, include her in a group he calls 'cheerfully postmodern'.

7 The Churchlands' style of philosophy is often referred to as 'eliminative materialism' (see P.M. Churchland 1989: 1–122).

8 In arguing for the superempirical value of simplicity, Churchland opts for the employment of minimal networks (181). I argue against them in Chapter 5.

9 I analyse this essay, entitled 'Racism's Last Word' (Derrida 1985), in a forthcoming article (Cilliers 1998).

8 AFTERWORD: UNDERSTANDING COMPLEXITY

1 See the Afterword to *Limited Inc.* (Derrida 1988) for this response.

Bibliography

Aleksander, I. and Taylor, J. (eds) (1992) *Artificial Neural Networks, 2: Proceedings of the 1992 International Conference on Artificial Neural Networks (ICANN-92)*. Amsterdam: North-Holland.

Argyros, A.J. (1991) *A Blessed Rage for Order: Deconstruction, Evolution, and Chaos*. Ann Arbor: University of Michigan Press.

Austin, J.L. (1980) *How to Do Things with Words*. 2nd edn. Oxford: Oxford University Press.

Axelrod, R. (1984) *The Evolution of Cooperation*. New York: Basic Books.

Bak, P. and Chen, K. (1991) Self-organized criticality. *Scientific American*, January, pp. 26–33.

Bass, A. (1984) The double game: An introduction. In J.H. Smith and W. Kerrigan (eds), *Taking Chances: Derrida, Psychoanalysis and Literature*. Baltimore: Johns Hopkins University Press, pp. 66–85.

Baudrillard, J. (1984) The precession of simulacra. In B. Wallis (ed.), *Art after Modernism*. New York: New Museum of Contemporary Art, pp. 253–281.

—— (1988) *The Ecstasy of Communication*. New York: Semiotext(e).

Bauman, Z. (1992) *Intimations of Postmodernity*. London: Routledge.

—— (1993) *Postmodern Ethics*. Oxford: Blackwell.

Bechtel, W. (1987) Connectionism and philosophy of mind: An overview. *Southern Journal of Philosophy*, Vol. XXVI (Supplement), pp. 17–41.

Bierwisch, M. (1990) Perspectives on mind, brain and language: Linguistics as a cognitive science or touring the Chinese Room again. In A. Burkhardt (ed.), *Speech Acts, Meaning and Intentions*. Berlin: Walter de Gruyter, pp. 291–428.

Blackwell, R.J. (1976) A structuralist account of scientific theories. *International Philosophical Quarterly*, Vol. 16 , pp. 263–274.

Brooks, R.A. (1991) Intelligence without representation. *Artificial Intelligence*, Vol. 47, pp. 139–159.

Burkhardt, A. (ed.) (1990) *Speech Acts, Meaning and Intention: Critical Approaches to the Philosophy of John R. Searle*. Berlin: Walter de Gruyter.

Chaitin, G.L.J. (1975) Randomness and mathematical proof. *Scientific American*, May, pp. 47–52.

—— (1987) *Algorithmic Information Theory*. Cambridge: Cambridge University Press.

Chandrasekaran, B., Goel, A.K. and Allemang, D. (1988) Connectionism and information processing abstractions. *AI Magazine*, Winter, pp. 24–34.

Changeaux, J.-P., Heidemann, T. and Patte, P. (1984) Learning by selection. In P. Marler and H.S. Terrace (eds), *The Biology of Learning*. Berlin: Springer-Verlag, pp. 115–133.

Chomsky, N. (1957) *Syntactic Structures*. The Hague: Mouton.

—— (1972) *Language and Mind*. Enlarged edn. New York: Harcourt Brace Jovanovich, Inc.

—— (1980) *Rules and Representations*. New York: Columbia University Press.

Churchland, P.M. (1984) *Matter and Consciousness*. Cambridge, Mass.: MIT Press.

—— (1989) *A Neurocomputational Perspective: The Nature of Mind and the Structure of Science*. Cambridge, Mass.: MIT Press.

Churchland, P.M. and Churchland, P.S. (1990) Could a machine think? *Scientific American*, January, pp. 26–31.

Churchland, P.S. (1986) *Neurophilosophy. Towards a Unified Science of the Mind/Brain*. Cambridge, Mass.: MIT Press.

Churchland, P.S. and Sejnowski, T.J. (1992) *The Computational Brain*. Cambridge, Mass.: MIT Press.

Cilliers, F.P. (1990) The brain, the mental apparatus and the text: A post-structural neuropsychology. *South African Journal of Philosophy*, Vol. 9, No. 1 (February), pp. 1–8.

—— (1998) On Derrida and apartheid. *South African Journal of Philosophy*, Vol. 17, No. 1. Forthcoming.

Clapin, H. (1991) Connectionism isn't magic. *Minds and Machines*, Vol. 1, pp. 167–184.

Clark, A. and Lutz, R. (1992) *Connectionism in Context*. London: Springer-Verlag.

Clark, T. (1985) Computers as universal mimics: Derrida's question of mimesis and the status of 'artificial intelligence'. *Philosophy Today*, Winter, pp. 303–318.

Cornell, D. (1992) *The Philosophy of the Limit*. London: Routledge.

Culler, J. (1976) *Saussure*. London: Fontana Press.

—— (1983) *On Deconstruction*. London: Routledge and Kegan Paul.

Cummins, R. (1991) Form interpretation, and the uniqueness of content: Response to Morris (1991). *Minds and Machines*, Vol. 1, pp. 31–42.

Denning, P.J. (1990) Is thinking computable? *American Scientist*, Vol. 78 (March–April), pp. 100–102.

Derrida, J. (1973) *Speech and Phenomena, and Other Essays on Husserl's Theory of Signs*. Evanston, Ill.: Northwestern University Press.

—— (1976) *Of Grammatology*. Baltimore: Johns Hopkins University Press.

—— (1978) *Writing and Difference*. Chicago: University of Chicago Press.

—— (1981) *Positions*. Chicago: University of Chicago Press.

—— (1982) *Margins of Philosophy*. Brighton: Harvester Press.

—— (1983) The principle of reason: The university in the eyes of its pupils. *Diacritics*, Fall, pp. 3–20.

—— (1985) Racism's last word. *Critical Inquiry*, Autumn, pp. 290–292.

—— (1988) *Limited Inc*. Evanston, Ill.: Northwestern University Press.

Derthick, M. (1990) Review of S. Pinker and J. Mehler, 1988: *Connections and Symbols* (MIT Press, Cambridge, MA). *Artificial Intelligence*, 43 (1990), pp. 251–265.

Dreyfus, H.L. and Dreyfus, S.E. (1986) *Mind over Machine: The Power of Human Intuition and Expertise in the Era of the Computer*. New York: Free Press.

Eco, U. (1987) *Travels in Hyperreality*. London: Picador.

Edelman, G.M. (1987) *Neural Darwinism: The Theory of Neuronal Group Selection*. New York: Basic Books.

Feyerabend, P. (1975) *Against Method: Outline of an Anarchistic Theory of Knowledge*. London: Verso.

Flanagan, S. (1990) *Hildegard of Bingen. A Visionary Life*. London: Routledge.

Fodor, J.A. (1975) *The Language of Thought*. New York: Thomas Crowell.

—— (1981) *Representations*. Cambridge, Mass.: MIT Press.

Fodor, J.A. and Pylyshyn, Z.W. (1988) Connectionism and cognitive architecture: A critical analysis. In S. Pinker and J. Mehler (eds), *Connections and Symbols*. Cambridge, Mass.: MIT Press, pp. 3–71.

Freud, S. (1925) A note on the 'Mystic Writing-Pad'. In *Standard Edition*, Vol. 19. London: The Hogarth Press, pp. 225–232.

—— (1950) *Project for a Scientific Psychology*. In *Standard Edition*, Vol. 1. London: The Hogarth Press, pp. 281–397.

Garfinkel, A. (1987) The slime mold *dyctyostelium* as a model of self-organization in social systems. In F.E. Yates (ed.), *Self-Organizing Systems: The Emergence of Order*. New York: Plenum Press, pp. 181–212.

Gibson, J.J. (1979) *The Ecological Approach to Visual Perception*. Boston: Houghton Mifflin.

Globus, G.G. (1991) Deconstructing the Chinese Room. *Journal of Mind and Behaviour*, Vol. 12, No. 3, pp. 377–391.

Gödel, K. (1962) *On Formally Undecidable Problems*. New York: Basic Books.

Goodman, N.D. (1991) Review of Putnam (1988). *Minds and Machines*, Vol. 1, pp. 117–119.

Grossberg, S. (1982) *Studies of Mind and Brain*. Dordrecht: D. Reidel.

—— (ed.) (1987) *The Adaptive Brain*. 2 vols. Amsterdam: North-Holland.

—— (ed.) (1988) *Neural Networks and Natural Intelligence*. Cambridge, Mass.: MIT Press.

Guenthner, F., Lehman, H. and Schönfeld, W. (1986) A theory for the representation of knowledge. *IBM Journal of Research and Development*, Vol. 30, No. 1 (January), pp. 39–56.

Harland, R. (1987) *Superstructuralism: The Philosophy of Structuralism and Post-Structuralism*. London: Methuen.

Harnad, S. (1989) Minds, machines and Searle. *Journal for Experimental and Theoretical Artificial Intelligence*, Vol. 1, pp. 5–25.

Haugeland, J. (1981) *Mind Design: Philosophy, Psychology, Artificial Intelligence*. Montgomery, Ala.: Bradford Books.

—— (1985) *Artificial Intelligence: The Very Idea*. Cambridge, Mass.: MIT Press.

Hebb, D.O. (1949) *The Organization of Behaviour*. New York: Wiley.

Hecht-Nielsen, R. (1992) The munificence of high dimensionality. In I. Aleksander and J. Taylor (eds), *Artificial Neural Networks, 2: Proceedings of the 1992 International Conference on Artificial Neural Networks (ICANN–92)*. Amsterdam: North-Holland, pp. 1017–1030.

Hesse, M. (1988) Theories, family resemblances and analogy. In D.H. Helman (ed.), *Analogical Reasoning*. Dordrecht: Kluwer Academic Press, pp. 317–340.

—— (1992) Models, metaphors and truth. In F.R. Akkersmit and J.J.A. Mooij (eds), *Knowledge and Language III*. Dordrecht: Kluwer Academic Press, pp. 49–66.

Hirose, Y., Koichi, Y. and Hijiya, S. (1991) Back-propagation algorithm which varies the number of hidden units. *Neural Networks*, Vol. 4, No. 1, pp. 61–66.

Hofstadter, D.R. (1980) *Gödel, Escher, Bach: An Eternal Golden Braid*. Harmondsworth: Penguin Books.

Hofstadter, D.R. and Dennett, D.C. (eds) (1982) *The Mind's I: Fantasies and Reflections on Self and Soul*. Harmondsworth: Penguin Books.

Horgan, T. and Tienson, J. (1987) Settling into a new paradigm. *Southern Journal of Philosophy*, Vol. XXVI (Supplement), pp. 97–113.

Hornick, K., Stinchcombe, M. and White, H. (1989) Multilayer feedforward networks are universal approximators. *Neural Networks*, Vol. 2, No. 5, pp. 359–366.

Jen, E. (ed.) (1990) *1989 Lectures in Complex Systems*. Redwood City, Calif.: Addison-Wesley.

Judd, S. (1992) Why are neural networks so wide? In I. Aleksander and J. Taylor (eds), *Artificial Neural Networks, 2: Proceedings of the 1992 International Conference on Artificial Neural Networks (ICANN–92)*. Amsterdam: North-Holland, pp. 45–52.

Katz, B.F. and Dorfman, M.H. (1992) The neural dynamics of conversational coherence. In A. Clark and R. Lutz (eds), *Connectionism in Context*. London: Springer-Verlag, pp. 167–181.

Kauffman, S.A. (1991) Antichaos and adaptation. *Scientific American*, August, pp. 64–70.

—— (1993) *The Origins of Order: Self-Organisation and Selection in Evolution*. New York: Oxford University Press.

—— (1995) *At Home in the Universe: The Search for Laws of Complexity*. London: Viking Press.

Kohonen, T. (1988) *Self-Organization and Associative Memory*. 2nd edn. Berlin: Springer-Verlag.

Kolen, J.F. and Goel, A.K. (1991) Learning in parallel distributed processing networks: Computational complexity and information content. *IEEE Transactions on Systems Man and Cybernetics*, Vol. 21, No. 2 (March–April), pp. 359–367.

Krohn, W. and Küppers, G. (1989) Self-organization: A new approach to evolutionary epistemology. In K. Hahlweg and C.A. Hooker (eds), *Issues in Evolutionary Epistemology*. Albany, NY: State University of New York Press, pp. 151–170.

Lawson, H. (1985) *Reflexivity. The Post-Modern Predicament*. London: Hutchinson.

Lewin, R. (1993) *Complexity: Life on the Edge of Chaos*. London: Phoenix.

Lloyd, D.E. (1989) *Simple Minds*. Cambridge, Mass.: MIT Press.

Luhmann, N. (1985) *A Sociological Theory of Law*. London: Routledge and Kegan Paul.

Lyotard, J.-F. (1984) *The Postmodern Condition: A Report on Knowledge*. Manchester: Manchester University Press.

McCulloch, W.S. and Pitts, W. (1943) A logical calculus of the ideas immanent in nervous activity. *Bulletin of Mathematical Biophysics*, Vol. 5, pp. 115–133.

Marletti, D. (1990) Congruence and modulation in propositional attitudes. In A. Burkhardt (ed.), *Speech Acts, Meaning and Intentions*. Berlin: Walter de Gruyter, pp. 279–299.

Minsky, M. and Papert, S. (1969) *Perceptrons*. Cambridge, Mass.: MIT Press.

Morris, M. (1991) Why there are no mental representations. *Minds and Machines*, Vol. 1, pp. 1–30.

—— (1992) Beyond interpretation. Reply to Cummins (1991). *Minds and Machines*, Vol. 2, pp. 85–95.

Mountcastle, V.B. (1978) An organizing principle for cerebral function: The unit module and the distributed system. In G.M. Edelman and V.B. Mountcastle, *The Mindful Brain*. Cambridge, Mass: MIT Press, pp. 7–50.

Münch, D. (1990) Minds, brains and cognitive science. In A. Burkhardt (ed.), *Speech Acts, Meaning and Intention*. Berlin: Walter de Gruyter, pp. 367–390.

Nicolis, G. and Prigogine, I. (1989) *Exploring Complexity*. New York: Freeman and Co.

Norris, C. (1992) *Deconstruction and the Interest of Theory* London: Leicester University Press.

Parushnikova, A. (1992) Is a postmodern philosophy of science possible? *Studies in the History and Philosophy of Science*, Vol. 23, No. 1, pp. 21–37.

Pattee, H.H. (1987) Instabilities and information in biological self-organization. In F.E. Yates (ed.), *Self-Organization: The Emergence of Order*. New York: Plenum Press, pp. 325–338.

Penrose, R. (1989) *The Emperor's New Mind*. Oxford: Oxford University Press.

Pribram, K.H. and Gill, M.M. (1976) *Freud's 'Project' Reassessed.* London: Hutchinson.

Prigogine, I. and Stengers, I. (1984) *Order out of Chaos: Man's New Dialogue with Nature.* London: Heinemann.

Putnam, H. (1988) *Representation and Reality.* Cambridge, Mass.: MIT Press.

Rapaport, W.J. (1986) Philosophy, artificial intelligence, and the Chinese Room argument. *Abacus*, Vol. 3, No. 4, pp. 7–17.

Rorty, R. (1980) *Philosophy and the Mirror of Nature.* Oxford: Blackwell.

Rosenblatt, F. (1958) The perceptron: A probabilistic model for information storage and organization in the brain. *Psychological Review*, 65, pp. 386–408.

Rosenfeld, I. (1988) *The Invention of Memory: A New View of the Brain.* New York: Basic Books.

Rouse, J. (1990) The narrative reconstruction of science. *Inquiry*, Vol. 33, No. 1, pp. 179–196.

—— (1991a) Philosophy of science and the persistent narratives of modernity. *Studies in History and Philosophy of Science*, Vol. 22, No. 1, pp. 141–162.

—— (1991b) The politics of postmodern philosophy of science. *Philosophy of Science*, Vol. 58, pp. 607–627.

—— (1996) *Engaging Science: How to Understand Its Practices Philosophically.* Ithaca, NY: Cornell University Press.

Rumelhart, D.E. and McClelland, J.L. (1986) *Parallel Distributed Processing: Explorations in the Microstructure of Cognition*, 2 vols. Cambridge, Mass.: MIT Press.

Saussure, F. de (1974) *Course in General Linguistics.* London: Fontana.

Schalkwyk, D. (1991) The meaning of wor(l)d: Value, sense, and reference in *Not Saussure* by Raymond Tallis. *Journal of Literary Studies*, Vol. 7, No. 3/4 (December), pp. 193–216.

Schrag, C.O. (1992) *The Resources of Rationality: A Response to the Postmodern Challenge.* Bloomington: Indiana University Press.

Searle, J.R. (1969) *Speech Acts. An Essay in the Philosophy of Language.* Cambridge: Cambridge University Press.

—— (1977) Reiterating the differences: A reply to Derrida. *Glyph*, Vol. 2, pp. 198–208.

—— (1979) Intentionality and the use of language. In A. Margalit (ed.), *Meaning and Use.* Dordrecht: Kluwer Academic Press, pp. 181–197.

—— (1980) Minds, brains, and programs. *Behavioral and Brain Sciences,* Vol. 3, pp. 417–457; Continuing Commentary in Vol. 5 (1982), pp. 338–348; Vol. 8 (1985), pp. 741–743.

—— (1982) The Chinese Room revisited. *Behavioral and Brain Sciences*, Vol. 5, pp. 345–348.

—— (1983) *Intentionality: An Essay in the Philosophy of Mind.* Cambridge: Cambridge University Press.

—— (1984) *Minds, Brains and Science.* Harmondsworth: Penguin Books.

—— (1985) Patterns, symbols, and understanding. *Behavioral and Brain Sciences,* Vol. 8, pp. 742–743.

—— (1990) Is the brain's mind a computer program? *Scientific American*, January, pp. 20–25.

Serra, R. and Zanarini, G. (1990) *Complex Systems and Cognitive Processes.* Berlin: Springer-Verlag.

Shannon, C.E. (1948) A mathematical theory of communication. *Bell System Technical Journal*, Vol. 27, pp. 379–423.

—— (1949) Communication in the presence of noise. *Proceedings of the Institution of Radio Engineers*, Vol. 37 (Jan.), pp. 10–21.

Sietsma, J. and Dow, R.J.F. (1991) Creating artificial neural networks that generalize. *Neural Networks*, Vol. 4, No. 1, pp. 67–79.

Smolensky, P. (1987) The constituent structure of connectionist mental states: A reply to Fodor and Pylyshyn. *Southern Journal of Philosophy*, Vol. XXVI (Supplement), pp. 137–161.

Staufer, D. (1987) Random Boolean networks: Analogy with percolation. *Philosophical Magazine B*, Vol. 56, No. 6, pp. 901–916.

Sterelny, K. (1990) *The Representational Theory of Mind*. Oxford: Blackwell.

Stofberg, J.A. (1988) Objectivity and the sociology of science. *South African Journal of Philosophy*, Vol. 7, No.4, pp. 213–225.

Toffoli, T. and Margolus, N. (1987) *Cellular Automata Machines: A New Environment for Modelling*. Cambridge, Mass.: MIT Press.

Touretzky, D.S. and Hinton, G.E. (1985) Symbols among the neurons: Details of a connectionist inference architecture. *Proceedings of the 9th International Joint Conference on AI*, Los Angeles, Calif., 18–23 August, pp. 238–243.

Turing, A. (1936) On computable numbers, with an application to the 'Entscheidungsproblem'. *Proceedings of the London Mathematic Society*, Series 2, 42, pp. 230–265.

—— (1950) Computing machinery and intelligence. *Mind*, Vol. LIX, No. 236. Reprinted in D.R. Hofstadter and D.C. Dennett (eds), *The Mind's I: Fantasies and Reflections on Self and Soul*. Harmondsworth: Penguin Books, 1982, pp. 53–67.

Von der Malzburg, C. (1987) Ordered retinotectal projections and brain organization. In F.E. Yates (ed.), *Self-Organizing Systems: The Emergence of Order*. New York: Plenum Press, pp. 265–277.

Von Foerster, H. (1985) Entdecken oder Erfinden – Wie lasst sich verstehen verstehen? In H. Gumin and A. Mohler (eds), *Einführung in den Konstruktivissmus*. Munich: Schriften der Carl-Friedrick-von-Siemens-Stiftung, pp. 27–68.

Wilden, A. (1984) *System and Structure: Essays in Communication and Exchange*, 2nd edn. London: Tavistock Publications Ltd.

—— (1987) *The Rules are No Game: The Strategy of Communication*. London: Routledge and Kegan Paul.

Index